OCS Study
MMS 2004-063

Coastal Marine Institute

High-Resolution Integrated Hydrology-Hydrodynamic Model: Development and Application to Barataria Basin, Louisiana

I0439053

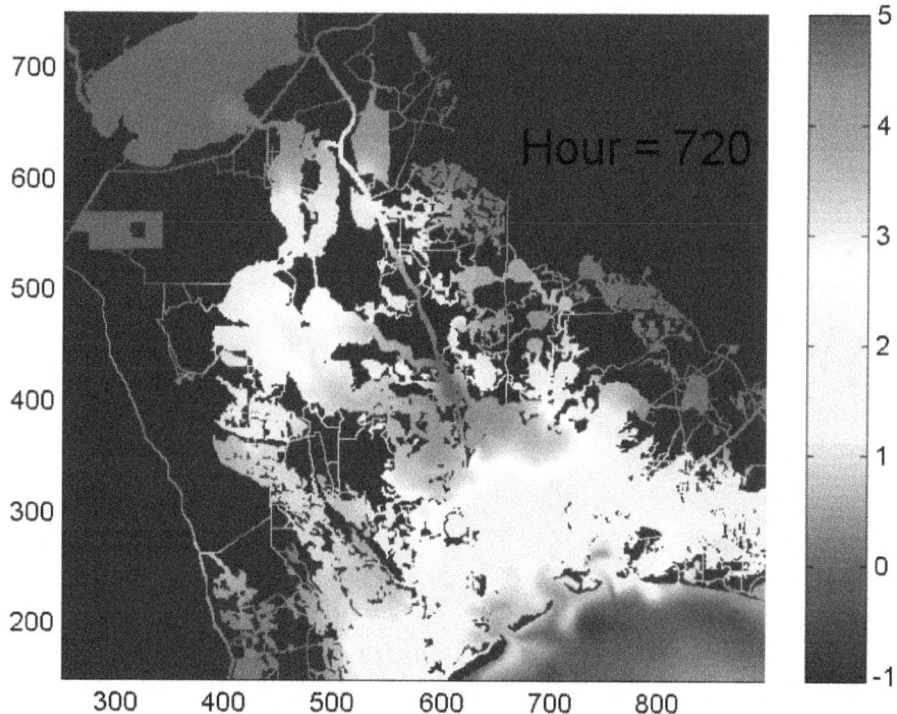

U.S. Department of the Interior
Minerals Management Service
Gulf of Mexico OCS Region

Cooperative Agreement
Coastal Marine Institute
Louisiana State University

OCS Study
MMS 2004-063

Coastal Marine Institute

High-Resolution Integrated Hydrology-Hydrodynamic Model: Development and Application to Barataria Basin, Louisiana

Authors

Dongho Park
Masamichi Inoue
William J. Wiseman, Jr.
Dubravko Justic
Gregg Stone

October 2004

Prepared under MMS Contract
14-35-0001-30951-19965
by
Coastal Marine Institute
Louisiana State University
Baton Rouge, Louisiana 70803

Published by

U.S. Department of the Interior
Minerals Management Service
Gulf of Mexico OCS Region

Cooperative Agreement
Coastal Marine Institute
Louisiana State University

DISCLAIMER

This report was prepared under contract between the Minerals Management Service (MMS) and Louisiana State University. This report has been technically reviewed by the MMS and approved for publication. Approval does not signify that the contents necessarily reflect the view and policies of the Service nor does mention of trade names or commercial products constitute endorsement or recommendation for use. It is, however, exempt from review and compliance with MMS editorial standards.

REPORT AVAILABILITY

Extra copies of the report may be obtained from the Public Information Office (MS 5034) at the following address:

U.S. Department of the Interior
Minerals Management Service
Public Information Office (MS 5034)
Gulf of Mexico OCS Region
1201 Elmwood Park Boulevard
New Orleans, Louisiana 70123-2394

Telephone Number: (504) 736-2519
1-800-200-GULF

CITATION

Suggested citation:

Park, D., M. Inoue, W. J. Wiseman, Jr., D. Justic, and G. Stone. 2004. High-Resolution Integrated Hydrology-Hydrodynamic Model: Development and Application to Barataria Basin, Louisiana. U. S. Dept. of the Interior, Minerals Management Service, Gulf of Mexico OCS Region, New Orleans, LA. OCS Study MMS2004 - 063. 74 pp.

ABSTRACT

This is the final report of our effort under Coastal Marine Environmental Modeling: Part III. Coastal Marine Environmental Modeling targets the development of numerical models of estuarine shelf interactions with the ultimate objectives of formulating a coupled hydrodynamic-ecological model that includes biological and sedimentological components. Under Part II, a two-dimensional depth-integrated hydrodynamic model, that includes baroclinic pressure gradient, was developed. This model has been applied to various estuaries in Louisiana, namely, Terrebonne/Timbalier Bay, Barataria Bay, Chandeleur-Breton Sound and Fourleague Bay. A simplified version of the hydrodynamic model has been coupled to a simple ecological model that includes suspended sediments, nutrients and phytoplankton, to simulate a spring bloom in Fourleague Bay. In this report, development of a high-resolution integrated hydrology-hydrodynamic model of Barataria Basin is presented. First, a hydrology model that explicitly accounts for the local hydrological cycle over the surrounding drainage basins for the Barataria Basin is developed. Using observed precipitation and estimated evaporation over the surrounding drainage basins, the hydrology model provides estimates of local runoff. The hydrology model is coupled to a high-resolution (O (100m)) two-dimensional depth-integrated hydrodynamic model of the Barataria Basin in order to simulate the hydrodynamic response of Barataria Basin to hydrological, tidal, and wind forcing. A flood event during tropical storm Allison in June 2001 resulted in significant rise in sea-level heights especially in the upstream region of the basin, thus, providing a rare opportunity to test the model. It is shown that the integrated model is capable of capturing a significant portion of the observed sea-level variations during the flood. The integrated model was also used to simulate a typical dry summer condition, namely the 30-day period during the summer of 1999. Despite the relatively crude salinity initial condition used (based on only eight observations), the model appears to do reasonable job of simulating time evolution of salinity fields inside the bay. The model was then used to simulate potential impact of freshwater diversions at Naomi, West Pointe à la Hache, and Davis Pond. Those simulation runs suggest that even at reasonable diversion rates, notable impacts on water level and salinity should be observable in the multiply connected channels through the marsh in the vicinity of operating diversion structures within several days of freshwater release, and after 15 days or so even in the downstream regions of the basin. The largest impact of diversions should be felt in the mid-bay region where the ambient salinity gradients are the steepest. It is notable that the diversion signal propagates at shallow-water wave speed, like a tidal bore, due to its mass flux, that is much faster than the diffusion time-scale suggested for mixing of two water masses in estuaries (e. g., Elliot and Reid, 1976). It is interesting to note that even after day 30, some isolated areas still remain without noticeable influence of the diversion. Those observations highlight the need to use high model resolution, sufficiently high enough to resolve many of the important complex morphological features of the basin in order to achieve reasonable simulation capability for morphologically complex basins such as Barataria Basin. With the availability of the integrated hydrology-hydrodynamic model, the foundation has been laid toward establishing modeling capability that could be usable for realistic management purposes.

TABLE OF CONTENTS

LIST OF FIGURES

LIST OF FIGURES
(continued)

LIST OF FIGURES
(continued)

LIST OF FIGURES
(continued)

LIST OF TABLES

ACKNOWLEDGMENTS

We would like to thank the Coastal Marine Institute at Louisiana State University that is funded by the Minerals Management Service for providing the necessary support for this project. We would like to acknowledge assistance provided by many people including Christopher M. Swarzenski and Erick M. Swenson in providing field data and many insights into hydrology and hydrodynamics of Barataria Basin. Invaluable suggestions and guidance on many meteorological problems were provided by S. A. Hsu. We thank the National Oceanic and Atmospheric Administration, the U. S. Army Corps of Engineers, the United States Geological Survey, and the Louisiana Department of Natural Resources for providing many of the data sets used.

CHAPTER 1

FORMULATION OF AN INTEGRATED
HYDROLOGY-HYDRODYNAMIC MODEL

1.1 Introduction

Barataria Basin is located immediately west of the Mississippi River delta and is bounded on the north and east by the Mississippi River, on the west by Bayou Lafourche, and on the south by the Gulf of Mexico (Fig. 1-1). The total area of the basin covers approximately $6,300 \, km^2$. The basin is an irregularly shaped area bounded on each side by a levee formed by the present and a former channel of the Mississippi River. A chain of barrier islands separates the basin from the Gulf of Mexico. In the northern half of the basin, several large lakes occupy the sump position.

During the last several hundred years, in coastal Louisiana, land building processes have been greatly reduced, while the erosion rate continues and probably has accelerated due to the activities of man (Van Sickle et al., 1976). The primary pattern of land loss in the Louisiana coastal zone results from the submergence of coastal marshes and subsequent conversion to open water (Turner, 1990). Within the Barataria Basin, wetland loss rates averaged nearly $23.1 \, km^2$ per year between 1974 and 1990 (Louisiana Coastal Wetlands Conservation and Restoration Task, 1993). This high rate appears to be due to a combination of natural processes such as subsidence, sea-level rise, canal dredging, and the river funneling sediments across the continental shelf making them unavailable for coastal marshes (Bowman et al. 1995). Of the numerous factors contributing to this loss, perhaps the leveeing of the Mississippi River for flood control has had the most far-reaching impact. Artificial flood control levees were constructed along the Mississippi River and in 1904 Bayou Lafourche was artificially dammed. Ever since construction of the flood control levee along the Mississippi River, rainfall had been the main source of freshwater to the Barataria Basin. Only a small amount of riverine input, designed to mimic a natural crevasse, was introduced into the basin's wetlands through the recently completed siphons at Naomi and West Pointe à la Hache. These have been working at a maximum pumping rate of $60 \, m^3 \, s^{-1}$ of freshwater at each site. Another diversion site, Davis Pond, was recently opened with a maximum design-pumping rate of $300 \, m^3 \, s^{-1}$ of freshwater.

A major consequence of man-made freshwater diversions in estuarine environments such as Barataria Basin is its impact on salinity distribution. Salinity gradients, such as those within Barataria and Terrebonne estuaries have a significant influence on the distribution of estuarine flora and fauna (Melancon et al., 1994). For example, the optimum salinity range for natural oyster growth and survival in Louisiana waters is 5 to 15 ppt (Galtsoff, 1964). Consequently, most oyster reefs are limited to the mid-regions of estuaries, away from the low salinity waters of the upper estuaries and the high salinity waters of the lower estuaries (Melancon et al., 1994). Another pressing issue for the state of Louisiana is a potential impact of salinity alteration resulting from man-made freshwater diversion in promoting mosquito-borne disease. A recent

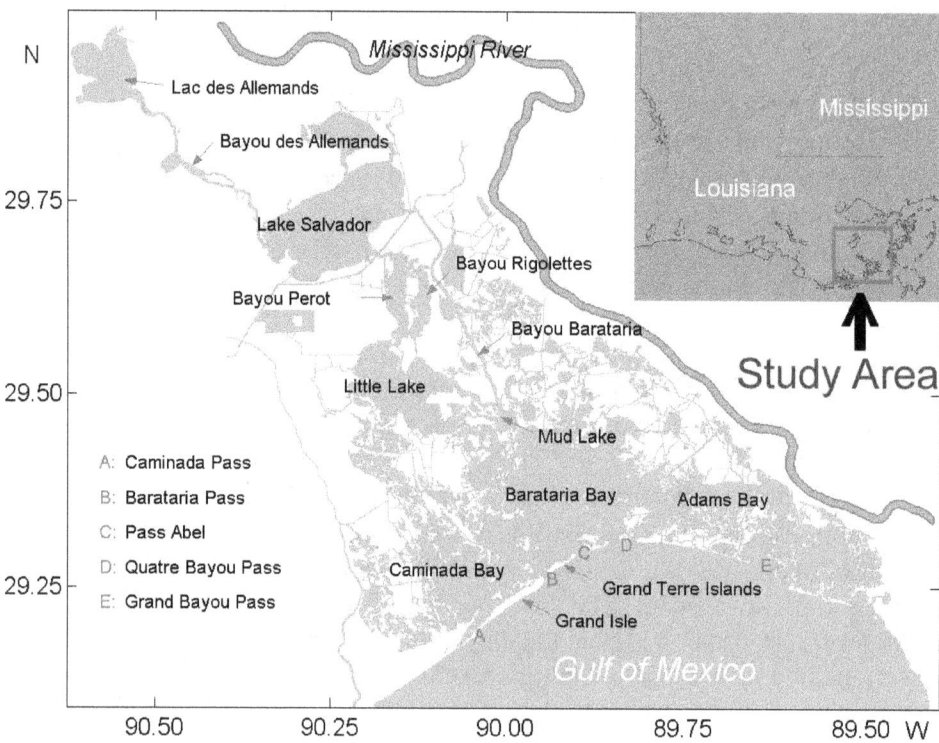

Figure 1-1. Study area and the model domain used. The southern boundary is open.

field study carried out by a Tulane University graduate student found increasing activities of salt marsh mosquitoes, a primary carrier of the West Nile virus, in freshwater areas impacted by the Davis Pond diversion (Sunday Advocate, March 23, 2003).

Tides in this region are small and diurnal (Marmer, 1954). However, the associated tidal currents contribute significantly to the exchange of salt between Barataria Basin and the adjacent Gulf of Mexico. Because of their predictability, these tidal flows are particularly important during the summer months when wind forcing is characteristically weak. Although the major water level fluctuations in Barataria Basin are governed by the diurnal tide at high frequencies, the wind controls the time-averaged estuarine water level on time-scales of a few days. In shallow water, such as in Louisiana coastal areas, the effect of wind stress usually overpowers the effects of the accompanying atmospheric pressure system (Byrne et al., 1976). Strong winds from the south "pile up" water along the coast, forcing water into the estuaries and raising water level about 0.3~0.5 m above normal. Conversely, winds from the north force water out of the estuaries depressing the water levels 0.3~0.5 m below normal (Swenson and Turner, 1998).

The summer weather encountered along coastal Louisiana is usually dominated by the Bermuda High Pressure system, which puts the Louisiana coast under the influence of synoptic winds with southerly and easterly components. The winter, on the other hand, is characterized by a greater percentage of winds out of the east and north dominated by cold front passages.

Barrett (1971) and Gagliano et al. (1973) described an inverse relation between Mississippi River flow and coastal salinities in Louisiana, "Salinity in Louisiana coastal waters is seasonally variable, fluctuating primarily with seasonal changes in tide, rainfall, river discharge, and evaporation rate" (Barrett, 1971). The salinity signal is highly coherent with Mississippi River discharge on time scales of the order of a year (Wiseman and Swenson, 1989). Salt wedges and salinity stratification were found to be absent in most of coastal Louisiana's estuaries. Increasing salinity has been widely mentioned as a factor contributing to the loss of coastal wetlands in Louisiana. Wetland deterioration, channelization and increased tidal exchange are thought to be primary factors that could result in increased estuarine salinity (Wiseman and Swenson, 1989). Byrne et al. (1976) investigated long-term salinity trends using 14 to 19 years of data at three stations within Barataria Basin. They found that the trends vary in space, but generally, the highest values occurred during September to November, and the spring low had a three-month (February to May) lag between Grand Terre and Bayou Barataria. Wiseman et al. (1990b) studied salinity trends in Louisiana estuaries and concluded that a negative trend in mean salinity was presently occurring at the mouth of Barataria Bay.

Even though the study was unpublished due to the request of the Freeport Sulphur Company, one of the pioneers of hydraulic model studies for Barataria Bay was von Arx (1950). Kjerfve (1973) studied circulation and dynamics in Caminada Bay, using a set of linearized differential equations to investigate time-dependent behavior of the water surface; he found that the simulated slope vector reproduced measured conditions extremely well, as a function of time. Hacker (1973) developed two-dimensional, time-dependent transport equations to predict velocity profiles, tidal fluctuations, and temperature and salinity profiles. He found that the hydrodynamic model and energy transport model accurately predicted the dynamics of tidal fluctuations and velocity profiles and the time-varying temperature distribution, respectively, in the Barataria Bay. Banas (1978) computed salt and momentum balances in Barataria Bay. He found that the baroclinic pressure gradient and vertical eddy stress gradient were the dominant two forces in the lateral force balance, while the barotropic pressure gradient and Coriolis force prevailed in the longitudinal balance.

1.2   Hydrology and Freshwater Sources

Climatological salinity distribution in the Barataria Basin presented by Swensen and Turner (1998) (re-plotted in Figure 1-3) shows a wide salinity range going from freshwater in the upper bay to ~15 ppt in mid-bay and to ~25 ppt at the mouths of the bay. Apparently, freshwater input from the surrounding drainage basins contributes significantly, in particular, in the upstream part of the basin in order to maintain nearly fresh water salinity there. This is due to the high land to water ratio in the upstream compared to the downstream (Figure 1.2). Salinities in the downstream part gradually increase toward the open Gulf of Mexico salinities. Consequently, freshwater runoff from the surrounding drainage basins appears to be the most dominant fresh water source in the long-term climatological salinity distribution (Marmer, 1954; Kjerfve, 1973; Light et al., 1973; Butler, 1975; and Van Sickle et al., 1976).

Freshwater input into Barataria Basin is contributed largely by the following four sources (Table 1-1):

1) direct rainfall on the open water surface,
2) runoff of rainfall over the surrounding drainage basins,
3) man-made freshwater diversions, namely, Naomi Freshwater Diversion, West Pointe à la Hache and Davis Pond Freshwater Diversion from the Mississippi River, and
4) the Gulf Intracoastal Waterway as a conduit of freshwater from the Atchafalaya River, a major distributary of the Mississippi River.

Annual mean precipitation for the 30-year period 1970-1999 was reported to be 163.9 cm at New Orleans International Airport (Garoogian, 2001). Evaporation removes freshwater from open water surface. On a long-term (1961-1990) annual basis, precipitation over coastal Louisiana exceeds evaporation. In summer, evaporation often exceeds precipitation. Drier than-normal conditions generally result in higher salinities even in the upstream part of the basin (Lee, personal communication, 2002). Butler (1975) demonstrated that the low discharge into Lac des Allemands in July and August is the result of two different phenomena. Evapotranspiration normally exceeds rainfall during the summer, so swamp drainage, the major hydrologic input to the lake and bayous, is reduced. Furthermore, during the summer, Ekman convergence due to the prevailing southeasterly winds retards the flow of water from Bayou des Allemands. The flow is further retarded during the day because of the sea breeze effect. At night the flow direction is typically reversed in a gulfward direction due to the land breeze effect. These tendencies are, of course, modulated by tides.

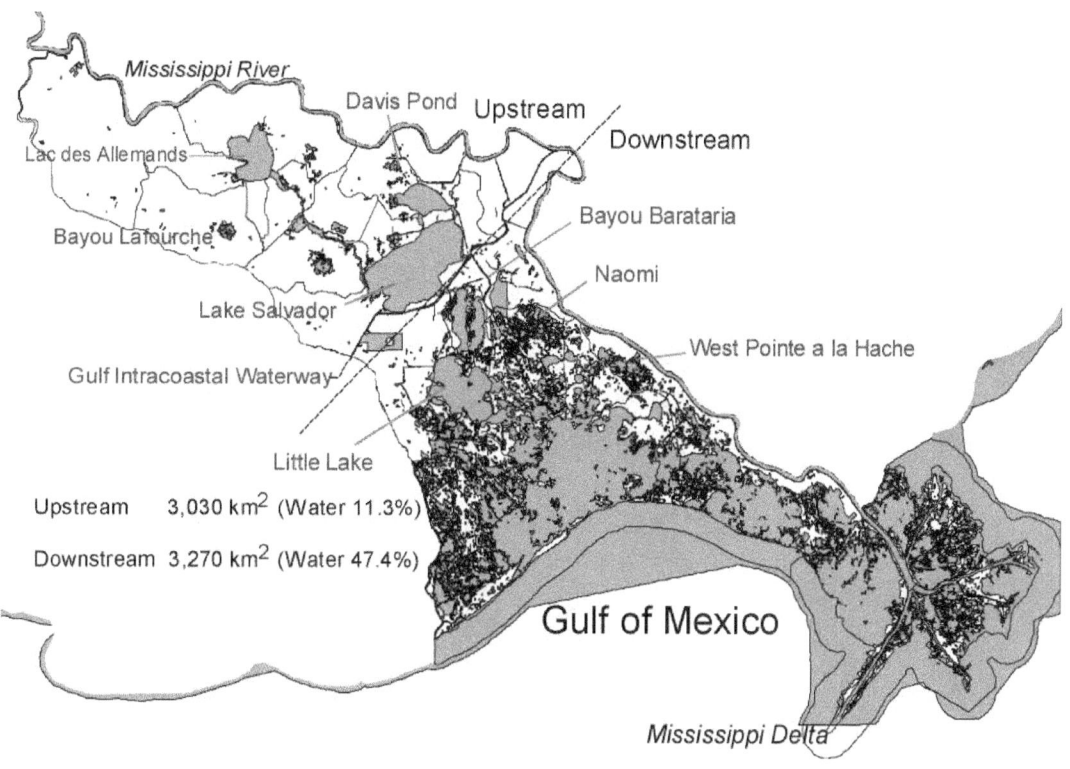

Figure 1-2. Barataria Basin including the surrounding drainage basins.

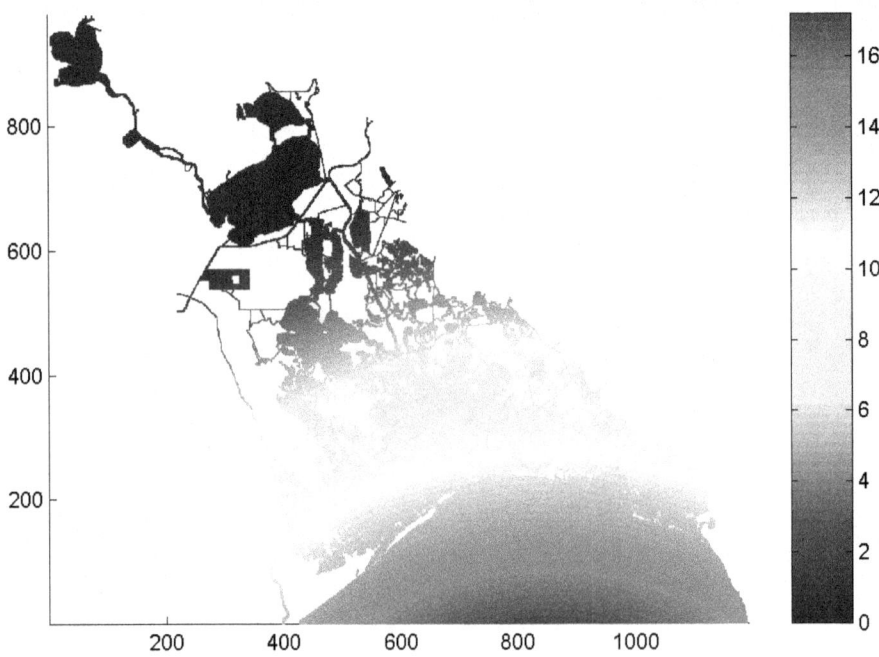

Figure 1-3. Climatological salinity distribution for the Barataria Basin (re-plotted from Swensen and Turner (1998)).

Table 1-1

Freshwater Sources in Barataria Basin System

Freshwater Sources	Location	Amount (m^3 sec^{-1})
Direct Rainfall	Rainfall on Water Surfaces	Variable with Rainfall
Runoff by Rainfall from Various Streams	64 Known Streams	Variable with Rainfall and Drainage Area
	522 Unknown Streams	
Diversion from	Naomi	60 at Maximum
	West Point a La Hache	60 at Maximum
	Davis Pond	300 at Maximum
Intercoastal Waterway	From West of Basin	50 on Average

Recent observations suggest that freshwater input from the Gulf Intracoastal Waterway averages ~60 m^{3}s^{-1} due to sea-level differences between the Barataria Bay and the neighboring Atchafalaya Bay that is impacted by the Atchafalaya River (Swarzenski, personal communication, 2002). It should be noted, however, that freshwater input from the Gulf Intracoastal Waterway could rival those at the man-made diversion sites (Swarzenski, personal communication, 2002).

1.3 Modeling Approach

Our previous research efforts to model circulation in Louisiana estuaries included applications of a two-dimensional depth-integrated hydrodynamic model to Terrebonne/Timbalier Basin (Inoue and Wiseman, 2000), Fourleague Bay (Wiseman and Inoue, 1993), Barataria Basin (Park, 1998; Inoue et al., 1998) and Chandeleur/Breton Sound (Inoue et al., 2001). In all those previous applications, the hydrodynamic model has been carefully tested and calibrated using the observed sea-level and/or current data. In order to simulate salinity distribution in Louisiana estuaries, an integrated hydrology-hydrodynamic model was developed (Park, 2002) to simulate the hydrological cycle depicted in Figure 1-4. Development and application of the integrated model for Barataria Basin are presented here. The hydrology model that explicitly accounts for freshwater runoff from the surrounding drainage basins is developed first. Then, the hydrology model will be coupled to a high-resolution version of the hydrodynamic model. The objective is to be able to estimate runoff given estimates of rainfall and evaporation, and to simulate hydrodynamics and salinity within the basin in response to freshwater input. The integrated model will be forced by observed tides coming from the Gulf of Mexico, local wind, rainfall and evaporation over the model domain, salinity estimated at the open boundary located offshore of the mouth of the bay. Estimated local precipitation and evaporation over the model domain based on actual meteorological observations provide hydrological forcing to the hydrological model, which in turn simulates local runoff into the hydrodynamic model (Figure 1-5). The integrated hydrology-hydrodynamic model will be used to simulate salinity variations within the Barataria Basin for a typical dry summer in Louisiana, July 1999.

1.4 Freshwater Sources

1.4.1 Rainfall

Precipitation, as a function of time and space, is highly variable. For example, daily precipitation records at New Orleans Moisant Airport (MSY) and the Grand Isle C-MAN (GDIL1) station, that are separated by about 80 km, show the correlation coefficient of only $r^2 = 0.34$ in 1999 (Figure 1-6) and appears to vary seasonally (Park, 2002). There were only five stations where precipitation measurements were made in the vicinity of Barataria Basin. For this study, however, only the precipitation record from MSY was used for the following reason. The dominant upstream regions which account for 61% of total land are best represented by MSY

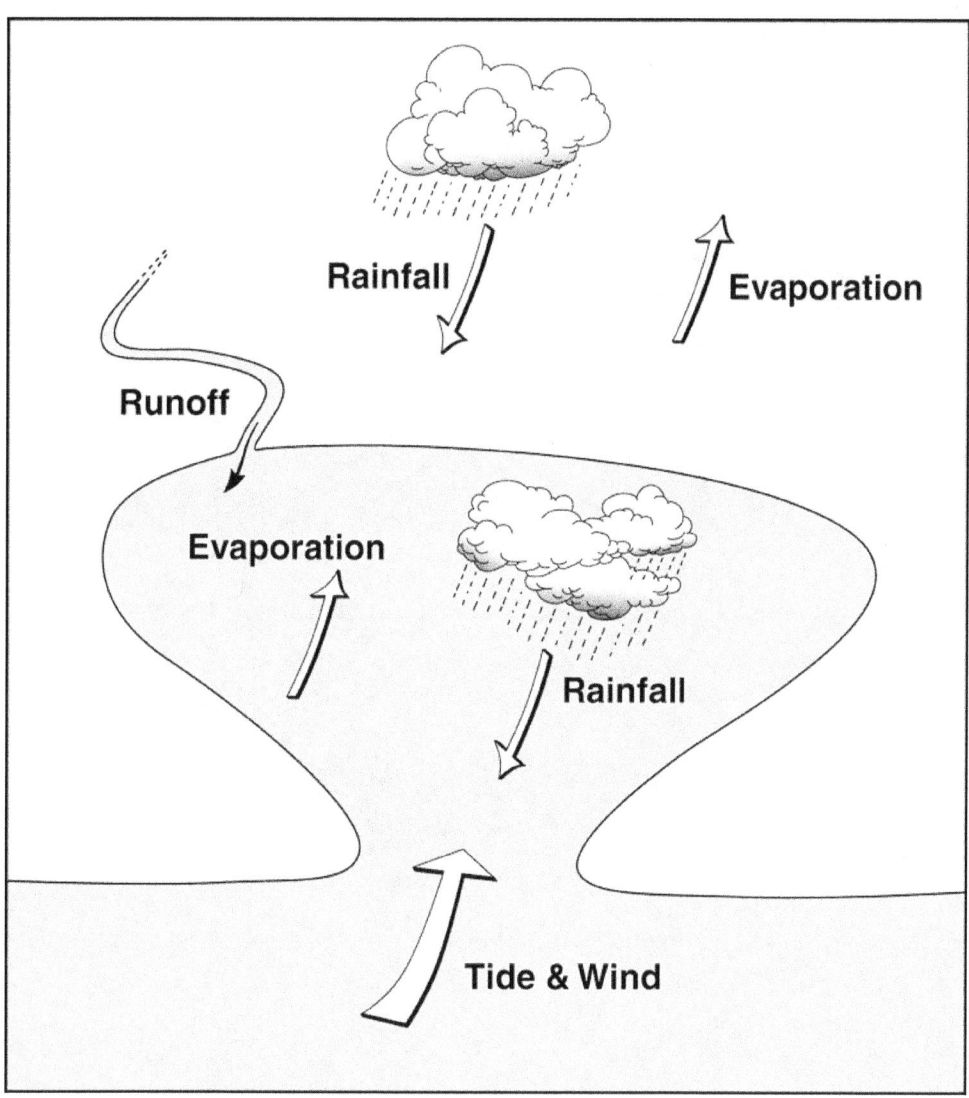

Figure 1-4. Schematic diagram illustrating hydrological cycle and forcing
functions for hydrodynamics in the Barataria Basin.

Integrated hydrology-hydrodynamic model

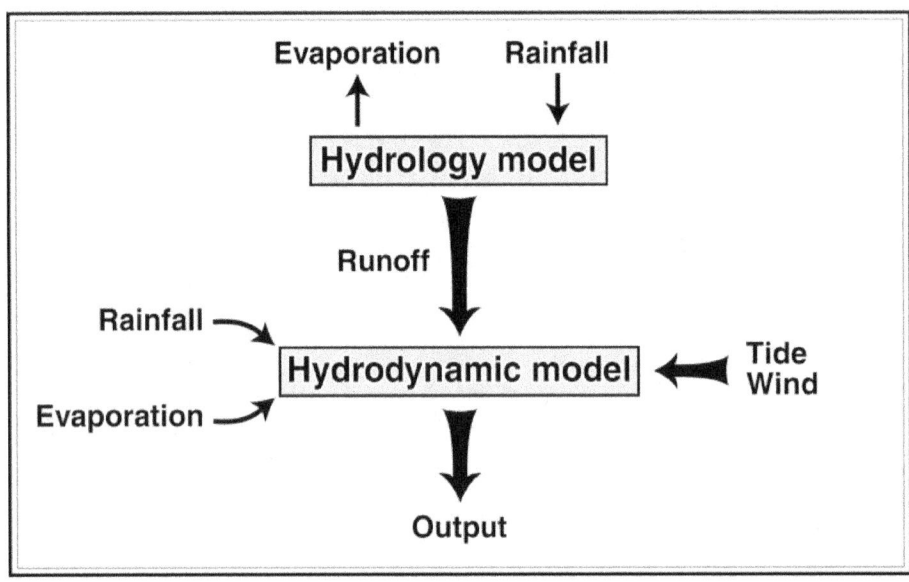

Figure 1-5. Modeling approach for an integrated hydrology-hydrodynamic model.

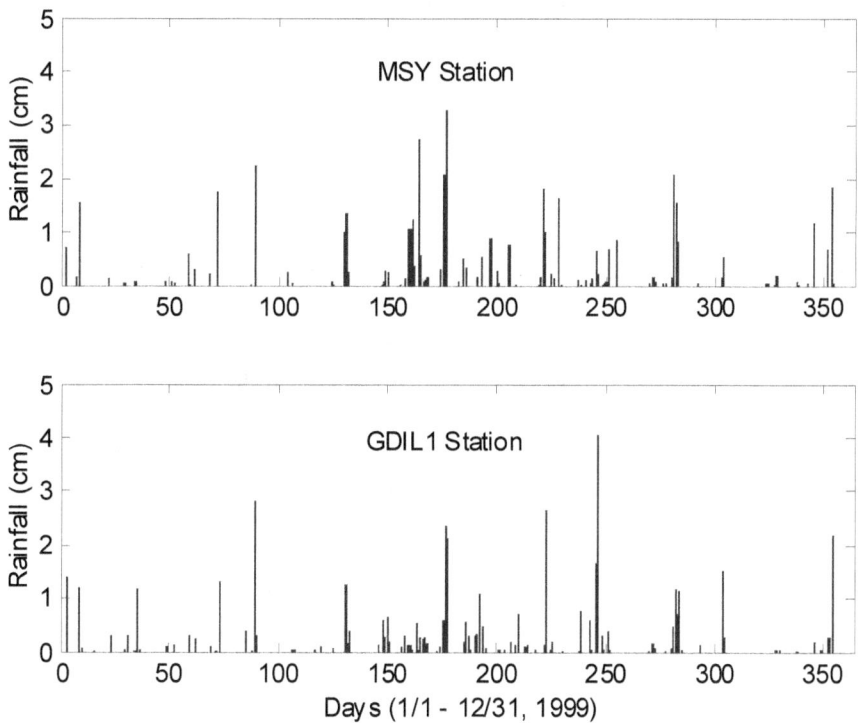

Figure 1-6. Daily precipitation at MSY (upper) and GDIL1 (lower) in 1999.

12

station. In addition, MSY was the only station where rainfall was measured at hourly intervals, a minimum temporal resolution required in the modeling in order to resolve short-duration but intense rainfall events that are common in Louisiana in summer. Therefore, uniform spatial distribution of precipitation over the entire domain was assumed based on the measurement at MSY station.

1.4.2 Evaporation

Methods used to estimate the amount of evaporation include: 1) measurement by evaporation pan, 2) empirical formulae, 3) water budget methods, 4) mass transfer methods, and 5) energy budget methods (Raudkivi, 1979). Near the Barataria Basin study area, pan measurements are available. Evaporation pan measurement is relatively simple and the results are in a reasonably constant ratio to evaporation estimates from large open water surfaces using other techniques. The measurements are relatively consistent from region to region. The evaporation is measured using a class A Pan at Houma and is only available at daily intervals, being too coarse to be comparable to hourly rainfall measurements (Figure 1-7). Therefore, the empirical formulae method, well suited for studying the Gulf coastal regions, was used in this study. The regional average evaporation is dependent primarily upon the energy available and vapor pressure gradients above the evaporating surface.

Latent heat flux occurs as a result of the transfer of water vapor from the ocean to the atmosphere. Latent heat flux due to evaporation, H_l, is estimated as (Roll, 1965)

$$H_l = L_T E = L_t C_E \rho (q_{sea} - q_{air}) U_{10} \qquad (1)$$

where L_T is the latent heat of vaporization, E is the evaporation rate, C_E is the latent heat coefficient, ρ is the air density, q_{sea} and q_{air} are the specific humidity for the sea and air, respectively, and U_{10} is wind speed at the 10 m reference height.

At the sea surface, the specific humidity, q_{sea}, is related to the saturation vapor pressure, e_{sea}, through (Hsu, 1988)

$$q_{sea} = 0.62(e_{sea} p^{-1}) \qquad (2)$$

where, $e_{sea} = 6.1078 \times 10^{[7.5 T_{sea}/(237.3 + T_{sea})]}$, p is atmospheric pressure, and T_{sea} is the sea surface temperature (^oC). Similarly,

$$q_{air} = 0.62(e_{air} p^{-1}) \qquad (3)$$

where, $e_{air} = 6.1078 \times 10^{[7.5 T_{dew}/(237.3 + T_{dew})]}$, and T_{dew} is the dew-point temperature (^oC).

Since we are dealing with heat loss from the sea to the air, the following values are used in our computations: $C_E = 1.12 \times 10^{-3}$ (Smith et al., 1994); $\rho = 1.2 kg\ m^{-3}$, and

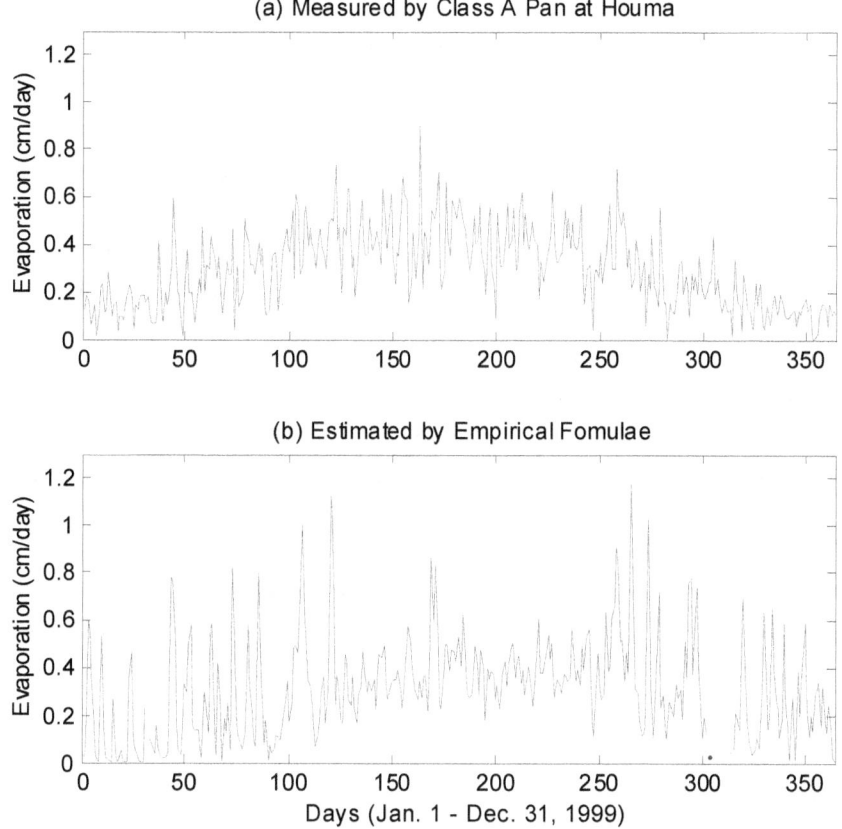

Figure 1-7. Measured evaporation at Houma (top) and estimated evaporation rate time series in 1999 from GDIL1 station (bottom).

$L_T = 2.5 \times 10^5 J \ kg^{-1}$ (Hsu, 1988). Note that a latent heat flux of $1 W \ m^{-2}$ is equivalent to an evaporation rate of $3.56 \times 10^{-3} cm \ day^{-1}$ (Colon, 1963).

Hourly measurements of atmospheric pressure, wind speed, sea surface temperature, and dew-point temperature available at GDIL1 station were all used to estimate evaporation. In 1999, which is considered to be a dry year, the total amount of evaporation estimated using the GDIL1 data was about 124 cm, which exceeded the total Class A Pan measured by nearly 10 cm. Figure 1-7 shows the estimated evaporation time series using GDIL1 station data. Evaporation was generally higher than the mean for the year 1999, with small variation, in summer. It was generally lower than the mean, but highly variable with several-day time scales, during the other seasons. Even though the estimated annual mean, 0.34 cm day^{-1}, is slightly higher than the measured mean, 0.32 cm day^{-1}, there are some seasonal differences. It should be noted that the measurement value is slightly higher on average during summer and exhibits lower fluctuations during the other seasons than the estimated evaporation rate due to several reasons. It has been found that cold fronts are the meteorological forcing agents affecting many air-sea interaction mechanisms, including evaporation and heat loss to the atmosphere from the Gulf of Mexico (e.g., Henry, 1979; Huh et al., 1984; Hsu, 1997).

1.4.3   Freshwater Diversion

Diversion structures provide a controlled flow of freshwater and nutrients from the Mississippi River into a target area in Barataria Basin. The essential goals of freshwater diversions were to manage the productivity of wildlife and fishery resources by controlling salinity and to maintain marsh elevation by introducing additional freshwater and sediments to the marsh (Roberts et al., 1992). Two freshwater diversions, Naomi and West Pointe à la Hache (Figure 1-2), currently were opened along the Mississippi River in 1992. The Naomi project area contains approximately 13,000 acres (5,261 ha) of intermediate and brackish marsh. The West Pointe à la Hache project area contains approximately 9,300 acres (3,764 ha) of open-water and 7,600 acres (3,076 ha) of brackish marsh. Both diversions have a maximum design-pumping rate of 60 m³ s⁻¹. Another diversion site, Davis Pond, was recently opened in April, 2002 with a maximum design-pumping rate of $300 m^3 s^{-1}$ of freshwater to preserve about 33,000 acres (13,354 ha) of marsh and benefiting 777,000 acres (31,444 ha) of marshes and bays (Boshart, 1998). The $119.6 million project, the world's largest freshwater diversion project, reintroduce fresh water, nutrients and sediment to the salt-threatened Barataria estuary, which stretches south to the Gulf of Mexico. Most of the diversion is expected to occur during the river's high-water season in the first half of the year. But the structure will be closed when storms and tides are expected to increase stages in Lakes Cataouatche and Salvador.

1.4.4 Intracoastal Waterway

Water flow in the Barataria Basin is often controlled by man-made navigation and drainage canals. Perhaps the best example is the Gulf Intracoastal Waterway. The Gulf Intracoastal Waterway is a coastal waterway route extending from Apalachee Bay, Florida to the Mexican border. As part of the Intracoastal Waterway system, the Gulf Intracoastal Waterway provides a practical navigation route along the coast of the Gulf of Mexico. Within Louisiana, the Gulf Intracoastal Waterway extends along the coast of the Gulf of Mexico from Lake Borgne to the Sabine River, a distance of 432 km. The Gulf Intracoastal Waterway is a conduit of freshwater and sediments to coastal Louisiana. The amount of freshwater and sediments introduced to coastal wetlands depends on the difference in head between the Lower Atchafalaya River and surrounding waters. The Lower Atchafalaya River varies in stage from year to year, depending upon what happens in the basin of the Mississippi River and Red River (Swarzenski et al., 1999). Recent observations suggest that freshwater input into the Barataria Basin from the Gulf Intracoastal Waterway averages ~50 m^3s^{-1} due to sea-level differences between the Barataria Bay and the neighboring Atchafalaya Bay that is impacted by the Atchafalaya River (Swarzenski, personal communication, 2002). It should be noted, however, that freshwater input from the Gulf Intracoastal Waterway could rival those at the man-made diversion sites, i. e., it needs to be included in any hydrological modeling effort to simulate freshwater runoff into the Barataria Basin. Swarzenski et al. (1999) found that the relationship with Larose water level and discharge in the Gulf Intracoastal Waterway, although positive, was less than linear. Water level 1.2 m above mean sea level at Larose is critical in terms of transport direction. For this study, long-term average flow, 50 m^3s^{-1}, in the Gulf Intracoastal Waterway from west of the Barataria Basin was assumed as a constant volume flux.

1.4.5 Runoff

Runoff enters the Barataria Bay estuarine system through a complex series of coastal swamps and wetlands, mostly from local precipitation. On a long-term (1961-1990) annual basis, precipitation over coastal Louisiana exceeds evaporation, thus, resulting in a net runoff into the Barataria Basin. Annual mean precipitation for the 30 years was reported as 160 cm (Baumann, 1987). In 1999, however, total precipitation was recorded as 114 cm due to the prolonged impact of the 1997-1998 El-Nino Southern Oscillation event, while the total amount of evaporation estimated using the GDIL1 data was about 124 cm. Hence, net freshwater input from the hydrological cycle must dictate the salinity distribution within the bay. Estuarine salinity decreases during periods of high runoff as the freshwater-saltwater interface moves down the estuary toward the sea, and it reverses when runoff decreases.

There are several previous studies of runoff from land in Barataria Basin. Light et al. (1973) developed a hydrologic model to analyze freshwater flow in the Barataria area using the watershed management unit method. This model used precipitation, evapotranspiration, and physiographic data to calculate annual discharge from Bayous Chevreuil, Boeuf, and des Allemands. The investigators also developed a mean annual precipitation map based on a long-term record (1945-1970), and found mean annual rainfall excess values of more than 50.8 cm (20 inches) in the upper-basin watershed. Similarly, Gagliano et al. (1973) modeled runoff from land and freshwater inputs to water bodies using the cell method and assuming water losses from the water surface, both open and vegetation-covered. They computed the mean geographical distribution of freshwater flow over the basin. Wax et al. (1978) produced a water budget based on climatic conditions to estimate periods of freshwater surplus and deficit for the Barataria Basin system.

Butler (1975) studied the characteristics of freshwater discharge and the drainage area near Lac des Allemands. He indicated that the freshwater inflow into Lac des Allemands was $42 \sim 54 \ m^3 \sec^{-1}$ under average flows and $\sim 80 \ m^3 \sec^{-1}$ under peak flow conditions. Wiseman and Swenson (1989) pro-rated this number to give a total runoff into the basin $\sim 150 \ m^3 \sec^{-1}$. Muller (1975) estimated that the freshwater input to the Barataria Basin was $12 \times 10^6 \ m^3$ per tidal cycle or $266 \ m^3 \sec^{-1}$. Howard (1982) estimated that the total precipitation over Barataria Basin was $21 \times 10^6 \ m^3$ per tidal cycle. Sklar (1983) produced an annual water budget for the upper portions of the Barataria Basin system based upon data from 1914 through 1978 and estimated that 40 % of the precipitation was available for runoff. His results showed that most of the surplus of freshwater occurred in winter, with deficits of freshwater most likely to occur during the summer. He also noted that deficits should not be expected to occur regularly, because precipitation is usually greater than evaporation. Recently, Swenson and Turner (1998) calculated a water budget using the 28-year average (1960~1988) of precipitation and found similar results to these of Sklar. For this study, freshwater input by rainfall was estimated simply by multiplying total amount of rainfall by the total drainage area. The long-term average rainfall is known to be $160 \ cm$, and the total drainage area is about $4,400 \ km^2$. Therefore, the freshwater input into the basin is $4,400 \ km^2 \times 1.6m \ year^{-1} = 1.15 \times 10^6 \ m^3$ per tidal cycle or $223 \ m^3 \sec^{-1}$, of which 25 percent flows to Lac des Allemands, which is comparable to some of the previous results.

Runoff modeling depends on the records from single point rain gauges, some of which provide estimates of rainfall intensities in time steps of one hour or better, while others provide daily estimates. In large catchments, models using a daily time step may be adequate for applications. In small catchments such as the one under consideration here, a daily time step may be longer than the storm response time of the catchment and finer time resolution may be required (Beven, 2000).

The water that contributes to streamflow may reach the stream channel by any of several paths from the point where it first reaches the ground as precipitation. The rainfall-produced runoff enters the system through a complex series of coastal swamps and wetlands, providing a mechanism for the slow release of fresh water over large wetland areas. The primary physical characteristics of the drainage basin are its area, shape, elevation, slope, orientation, soil type, drainage channel system, water storage capability and vegetal coverage (Raudkivi, 1979). Some water flows over the soil surface as surface runoff and reaches the stream soon after its occurrence as rainfall. Other water infiltrates through the soil surface and flows beneath the surface to the stream. The groundwater contribution to streamflow cannot fluctuate rapidly because of its very low flow velocity.

Because the relation between precipitation and runoff is influenced by various storm and basin characteristics, usually many approximate formulas are used to relate rainfall and runoff. Since most of the land area for the Barataria Basin is less than 1.5 meters above mean sea level (Gagliano et al., 1973) and covered with wetland that is saturated by water, no groundwater flow is assumed. Only surface flow is considered significant and is incorporated into the model. In many environments, evapotranspiration is as significant a contribution to the water balance as stream discharge. Thus, for extended periods of runoff simulation, it will be necessary to estimate actual evapotranspiration losses from a catchment area. However, due to the relatively small drainage areas considered here, resulting in relatively quick runoff and short periods of simulation, transpiration was ignored for this study. As a result, the following simple model was adapted to relate rainfall to runoff for any drainage basin,

$$\text{Runoff } (m^3 \text{hour}^{-1}) = (\text{Rainfall} - \text{Evaporation})(\text{m hour}^{-1}) \times \text{Area } (m^2). \quad (4)$$

Delineation of runoff catchment areas is one of the real challenges in modeling estuarine hydrology in South Louisiana. The availability of discharge data is important for the model calibration process. Streamflow rates may be determined from stream stage data calibrated using measurements of velocity and cross-sectional area. Butler (1975) estimated discharge rate, using this method, for two main streams, Bayou Chevreuil and Bayou Boeuf, draining into Lac des Allemands. Discharge data are, however, generally available at only a small number of sites in any region. Runoff modeling for sites where there are no available discharge data is a difficult task. Barataria Basin has numerous known or recognizable, as well as unknown, streams (Table 1-1) that vary considerably in size and length. It is impossible to install gauges to measure all their discharges. Even though most small streams are not immediately discernible on a map, one can assume that there should be runoff from all subaerial land.

In order to estimate the discharge rate from unknown and ungauged streams, the basin was divided into twenty-two watershed management units using a pre-existing watershed chart (A Digital Map of the State). The area of each watershed management unit was estimated (Figure 1-8). Each area segment contains land and water surface. Since the hydrodynamic model that was previously developed for shallow water accounts for freshwater input due to direct rainfall on the water surface separately, runoff estimates should only account for precipitation over land. Therefore, the area of water surface was subtracted from each watershed unit area. Based on a minimum two square kilometers of land area, at least 1 stream was arbitrarily specified for unknown streams. Known streams were also associated with drainage areas (Figure 1-9). Most unknown drainages are smaller than nine square kilometers. The length of unknown streams was estimated by assuming that all drainages are semi-circular in shape, i. e., length=$\sqrt{2 \times area / pi}$.

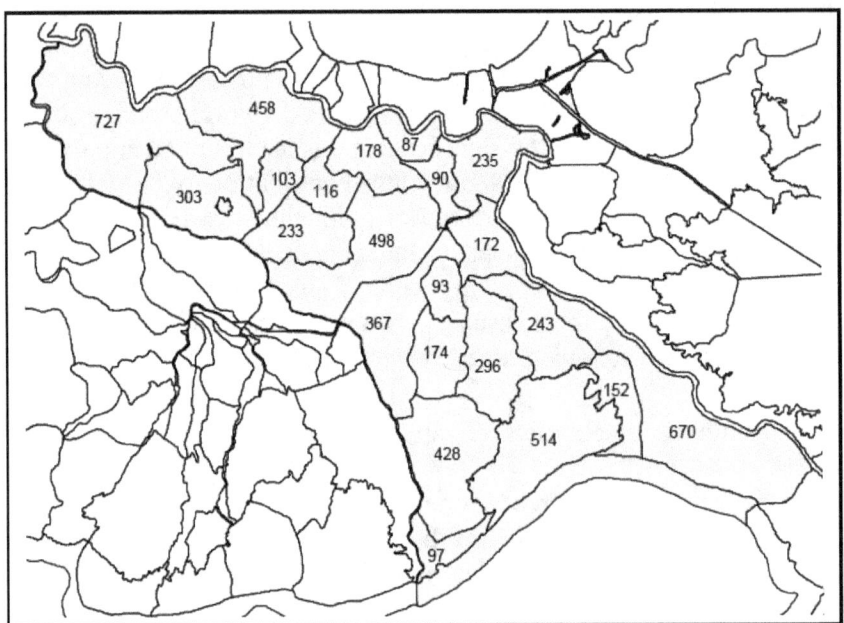

Figure 1-8. Twenty-two watershed management units of Barataria Basin.
The numbers on the map are the area of each subbasin in km^2.

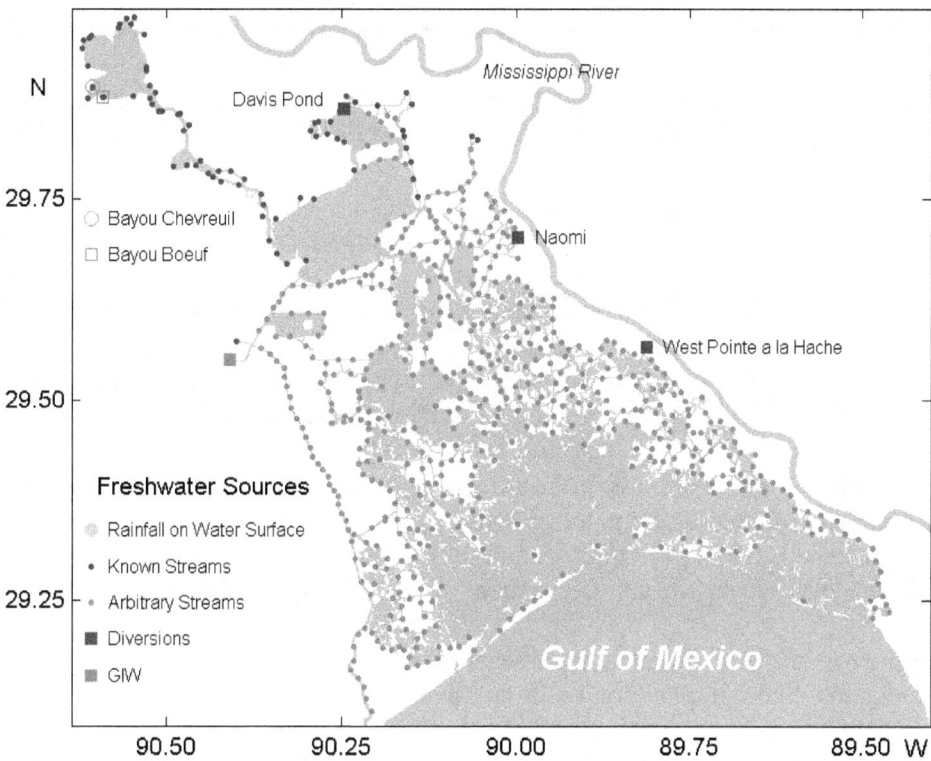

Figure 1-9. Freshwater sources defined in the hydrology model of the Barataria Basin.

The persistence time is defined as the time required for surface runoff to flow from the most remote point in a subbasin or subwatershed to the outlet (Walesh, 1989). All drainages were categorized based on their size and estimated persistence time (Table 1-2). The longest drainage system, Bayou Chevreuil (26 km), was known to have a 3-day (72 hours) persistence time. Other streams' persistence times were estimated by a linear extrapolation relative to the longest stream's persistence time.

Streamflow, at a given location on a watercourse, is represented by a hydrograph. The hydrograph produced in a stream is the result of various hydrologic processes that occur during and after any precipitation event. This continuous graph displays the properties of streamflow with respect to time, normally obtained by means of a continuous recorder that shows stage versus time, and then transformed into a discharge hydrograph by applying a rating curve. The shape of a hydrograph depends on precipitation pattern and characteristics and basin properties (Viessman et al., 1989). A stream's behavior is greatly affected by the characteristics of its watershed. For instance, the steadiness of the stream's flow at a given point is controlled by the area of the watershed upstream of the point. Typically, during a rainfall event, the hydrograph of an undisturbed stream rises fairly rapidly, and after reaching a peak value, falls off rather gradually. Streams differ from one another in many features besides area, though.

A complete analysis of the relation between rainfall and runoff, determining the characteristic shape of hydrographs for a basin, involves knowledge of the basin's physical, vegetative, and climatic characteristics, all of which affect the quantity of streamflow generated in a drainage basin. These parameters are not well known for the Barataria Basin. Another, simpler methodology must be employed for estimating the relationship between rainfall and runoff for the various sub-basins discharging into the Barataria Bay estuary.

The unit hydrograph, expected in response to a unit input of rainfall per unit area of marsh, may be considered to consist of three general parts: 1) the rising limb or concentration curve, 2) the crest segments, and 3) the recession curve or falling limb. Generally, the falling limb lasts longer than the rising limb, skewing the curve to the right. In order to estimate the total volume runoff entering the estuarine system, such a hydrograph should be multiplied by the amount of precipitation and the area of the sub-basin.

Using an one-sided filter, one can relate rainfall per unit time per unit area, x , to the resultant discharge from the sub-basin, y, as follows,

$$y(t_i) = a_1 x(t_{i-1}) + a_2 x(t_{i-2}) + \ldots + a_j x(t_{i-j}) \tag{5}$$

where j is the filter width, and a's are the filter coefficients. By selecting the filter width equal to the persistence time of the sub-basin, the effective runoff is limited within the persistence time. If water is conserved during runoff process, the following condition has to be satisfied.

Table 1-2

Drainage Types and Their Estimated Drainage Length and Persistence Time

Drainage Types	1*	2*	3*	4	5	6	7	8**
Drainage Size (km^2)	2	3-4	5-8	9-16	17-32	33-64	228	672
Drainage Length (km)	1.1	1.5	2.1	2.8	4.0	5.6	11.5	26.0
Persistence Time (Hour)	3.1	4.2	5.8	7.8	11.0	15.5	32.0	72.0
Number of Streams	373	124	25	32	26	4	1	1
Sub Total Area (km^2)	746	496	164	424	616	202	228	672

* unknown length of drainages
** known persistence time of drainage

$$a_1 + a_2 + a_3 + \ldots\ldots + a_j = 1 \tag{6}$$

In order to mimic the shape of a typical unit hydrograph response to a typical rainfall event, the following filter was adopted,

$$f(t) = \frac{1}{t^5} \exp\left(-\frac{2^2}{t} \right), \tag{7}$$

as shown in Figure 1-10. If the effective filter cutoff is taken as 5 in Figure 1-10, and noting that rainfall as well as runoff data are measured at hourly intervals (discrete time steps), one can select filter weights at discrete time intervals while maintaining the water conservation requirement. Thus, for eight different drainage basin sizes noted previously, appropriate filter weights can be selected. In carrying out actual computation, the filter width (i. e., the effective filter cutoff) can be set equal to the persistence time for any basin type specified in Table 2. It is noted that within Barataria Basin, Bayou Chevreuil and Bayou Boeuf (type 7 and 8, respectively) contribute almost 25 percent of freshwater to the entire Barataria Basin system.

1.5 Integration of the Hydrology Model and the Hydrodynamic Model

1.5.1 Numerical Model Formulation

The hydrology model developed in the previous section was integrated to a high-resolution depth-integrated two-dimensional model of estuarine circulation for the Barataria Basin. It was assumed that the use of two-dimensional depth-integrated equations for conservation of mass and momentum was adequate, considering the typically well-mixed water column due to wind and tidal stirring of the system (Inoue et al., 1998). The model used here is based on the model initially developed for other neighboring estuaries including Terrebonne-Timbalier Basin (Inoue and Wiseman, 2000), Fourleague Bay (Wiseman and Inoue, 1994), as well as Barataria Basin (Park, 1998). The description of the numerical model formulation being presented here comes from Inoue et al. (2001).

The model equations for conservation of mass and momentum including baroclinic pressure gradient written in Cartesian coordinates in terms of depth-integrated transport (e. g., Leendertse, 1967; Elliott and Reid, 1976) are;

$$\frac{\partial U}{\partial t} + \frac{\partial}{\partial x}\frac{U^2}{H} + \frac{\partial}{\partial y}\frac{UV}{H} - fV = -gH\frac{\partial \zeta}{\partial x} - \frac{1}{2}gH^2\frac{\partial \rho}{\partial x} - g\frac{\frac{U}{H}\left\{\left(\frac{U}{H}\right)^2 + \left(\frac{V}{H}\right)^2\right\}^{\frac{1}{2}}}{c^2} + \frac{\tau_x}{\rho} + A\nabla^2 U \tag{8}$$

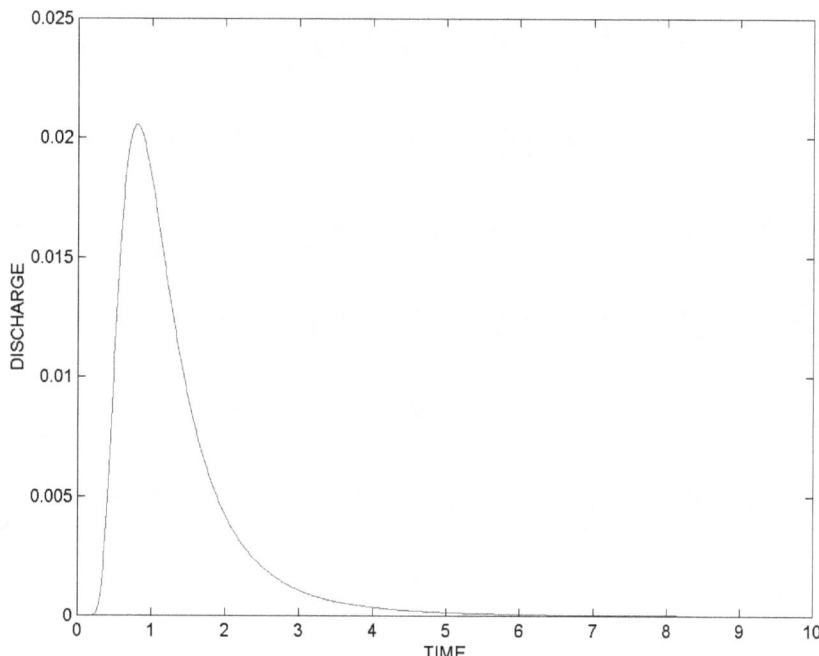

Figure 1-10. Function defined by $f(t) = \dfrac{1}{t^5} \exp\left(-\dfrac{2^2}{t} \right)$ used in this study to estimate the

shape of a unit hydrograph for various drainage basins in the Barataria Basin.

$$\frac{\partial V}{\partial t}+\frac{\partial}{\partial x}\frac{UV}{H}+\frac{\partial}{\partial y}\frac{V^2}{H}+fU=-gH\frac{\partial \zeta}{\partial y}-\frac{1}{2}gH^2\frac{\partial \rho}{\partial y}-g\frac{\frac{V}{H}\left\{\left(\frac{U}{H}\right)^2+\left(\frac{V}{H}\right)^2\right\}^{\frac{1}{2}}}{C^2}+\frac{\tau_y}{\rho}+A\nabla^2 V \tag{9}$$

$$\frac{\partial \zeta}{\partial t}+\frac{\partial U}{\partial x}+\frac{\partial V}{\partial y}=0 \tag{10}$$

$$\frac{\partial HS}{\partial t}+\frac{\partial HS}{\partial x}+\frac{\partial HS}{\partial y}=D_S\left(\frac{\partial H\frac{\partial S}{\partial x}}{\partial x}+\frac{\partial H\frac{\partial S}{\partial y}}{\partial y}\right) \tag{11}$$

$$\frac{\partial HT}{\partial t}+\frac{\partial HT}{\partial x}+\frac{\partial HT}{\partial y}=D_T\left(\frac{\partial H\frac{\partial T}{\partial x}}{\partial x}+\frac{\partial H\frac{\partial T}{\partial y}}{\partial y}\right) \tag{12}$$

where $U=\int_{-h}^{\zeta}u\,dz$, $V=\int_{-h}^{\zeta}v\,dz$, $H=h+\zeta$, $S=\frac{1}{H}\int_{-h}^{\zeta}s(z)dz$, and $T=\frac{1}{H}\int_{-h}^{\zeta}t(z)dz$

where t denotes time, x, y, and z are Cartesian coordinates, u and v denote velocity components in the direction of x and y, respectively, ζ is elevation of the free surface above mean sea level, h is the undisturbed depth of the water, f is the Coriolis parameter (assumed to be a constant), g is the acceleration due to gravity, τ_x and τ_y are the x and y components of wind stress, respectively, ρ is the density of water, s(z) and t(z) are depth-dependent salinity and temperature, respectively, A is the horizontal eddy viscosity, S is depth-averaged salinity, T is depth-averaged temperature, D_S and D_T are the horizontal eddy diffusivities for S and T, respectively, and C is the Chezy coefficient which is depth dependent. The bottom roughness is represented through Manning's n coefficient, such that the Chezy coefficient is evaluated as

$$C=\frac{1}{n}H^{\frac{1}{6}} \tag{13}$$

At land boundaries, no normal flow and no-slip boundary conditions are used. Wind forcing is assumed to be spatially uniform over the entire model domain. The model equations are discretized into a finite-difference formulation on the staggered mesh grid C of Arakawa (Mesinger and Arakawa, 1976). The Grammeltvedt C scheme (Grammeltvedt, 1969), which conserves mass and total energy, is employed. For time integration, the Leapfrog scheme is used with an Euler scheme inserted at regular time intervals to eliminate the computational mode due to the central time differencing. For numerical stability, the frictional terms are lagged in time.

1.5.2 Advection Scheme Used

One of the novel features of the model is the incorporation of a very accurate advection scheme. Traditionally, a simple centered-difference scheme has been used for advective transport in hydrodynamic models. This scheme induces so-called numerical dispersion, which causes nonphysical spatial oscillation in the tracer field (Hasumi and Suginohara, 1999). These oscillations could be damped out by using a large diffusion coefficient. However, as the model grid size is reduced to resolve finer and finer spatial scales, the use of large diffusion coefficients is no longer justified. Several schemes have been developed that have little numerical dispersion and a higher order of accuracy compared with the centered differencing scheme. They include the flux corrected transport (FCT) scheme of Boris and Book (1973), the Uniformly Third-Order Polynomial Interpolation Algorithm (UTOPIA; Leonard et al., 1993), the Quadratic Upstream Interpolation for Convective Kinematics (QUICK; Leonard, 1979) and the Multidimensional Positive Definite Advection Transport Algorithm (MPDATA; Smolarkiewicz, 1984).

In this study, advection scheme due to Takacs (1985) is adopted. This scheme is an accurate upstream scheme with very little numerical dispersion. In order to apply the Takacs scheme to a 2-D depth-integrated advection equation the following procedure is followed. The 2-D depth-integrated equation for advection is given by

$$\frac{\partial HS}{\partial t} + \frac{\partial US}{\partial x} + \frac{\partial VS}{\partial y} = 0 \tag{14}$$

where s is concentration of advected property. In order to apply the Takacs scheme to the above equation, it is necessary to account for volume changes into or out of the individual grid cells during each time-step, i. e., the following continuity equation needs to be solved at the same time,

$$\frac{\partial H}{\partial t} + \frac{\partial UH}{\partial x} + \frac{\partial VH}{\partial y} = 0 \tag{15}$$

1.5.3 Model Grid Setup

Most of the model bathymetry and morphology was taken from Nautical Charts (scale 1:80,000), topographic maps (scale 1:100,000) by U.S. Geological Survey, supplemented by recent satellite imagery. The morphology was modified using recent satellite images and aerial photos, since the most recent nautical charts (published in 1995) have not been changed since

1976. The coastal boundaries were approximated in the model as closely as possible. A spatially-uniform grid of 100 m was used.

1.5.4   Forcing Functions

The model was forced by realistic tides, salinity, water temperature, rainfall, local runoff, wind and freshwater diversion from the Mississippi River. Historical water level and salinity data from 1999 and 2001 collected by the United States Geological Survey (USGS) and the Department of Natural Resources, Louisiana (DNR), were obtained for Barataria Basin.

At the open boundary located at the southern end of the model domain, sea level height is specified. Open boundary conditions for salinity and temperature are set in such a way that for outflow (i. e., flowing toward the open boundary) the radiation boundary condition due to Carmerlengo and O'Brien (1980) is used, while for inflow (i.e., flowing into the model domain) a relaxation toward the specified value at the open boundary is applied.

Due to the lack of sea level height measurements near the southern open boundary, the water elevation recorder from site S1 was used to estimate sea level height at the southern open boundary. In addition, spatially uniform wind forcing based on wind measurements at GDIL1 (Grand Isle C-MAN Station) was included in the model.

An empirical relationship derived for the Barataria Basin (Hsu, 1996, personal communication) was used to convert from wind speed to wind stress. The relationships between, the wind stress, the shear velocity, U_* and the wind speed at 10 m height, U_{10}, for this study area are:

$$\tau = \rho_a U_*^2, \text{ and } U_* = 0.037 U_{10} - 0.03$$

where τ is the wind stress and ρ_a is the air density.

Due to the lack of salinity measurements near the southern open boundary, the salinity recorder from site S1 was used to estimate salinity values at the open boundary.
After initial calibration run, a Manning's n coefficient of 0.02 and a horizontal eddy viscosity used of 5 $m^2 s^{-1}$ were selected.

1.6   Testing of the Hydrology Model

Rarely, significant impact of local runoff manifests itself on sea-level heights in large estuaries such as Barataria Basin. Fortunately, in June 2001during tropical storm Allison, nearly 60 cm of rainfall fell, almost four-fold the long-term average for the month of July (Figure 1-11). Figure 1-12 shows three stations where sea level heights were measured during the storm, while Figure 1-13 shows observed wind at GDIL1. During the storm, wind was predominantly southerly until Hour 540. Significant impact of local rainfall due to the storm was evident in the sea-level records (Figures 1-14). Figure 1-14 also suggests that the predominant southerly wind during the storm (Figure 1-13) contributed toward raising sea level heights within the basin.

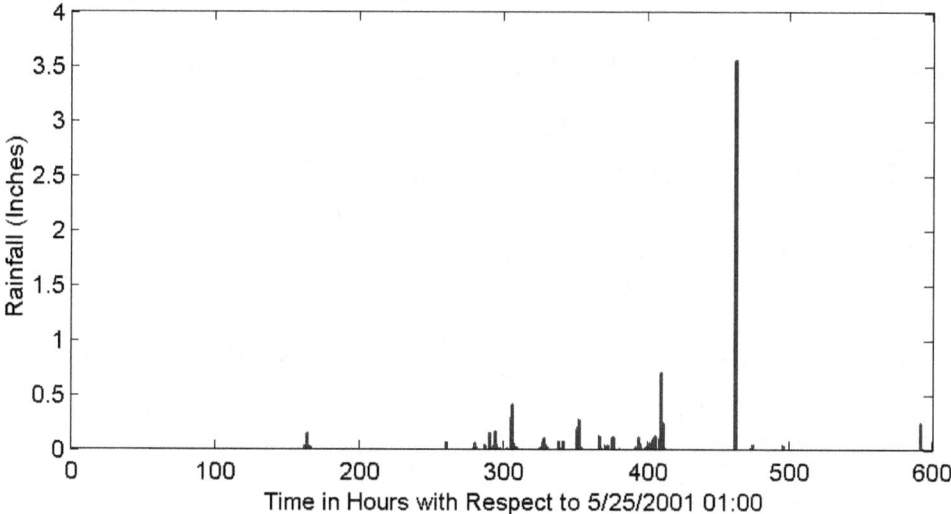

Figure 1-11. Rainfall measured at MSY during tropical storm Allison in June 2001.

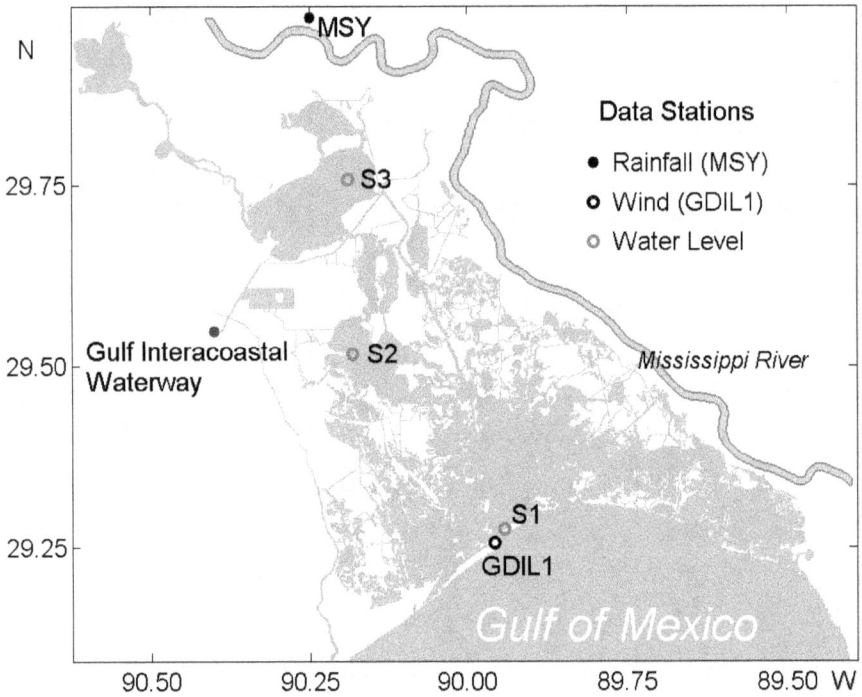

Figure 1-12. Sea-level stations, rainfall measurement site, and wind measurement site used in the flood simulation during Allison.

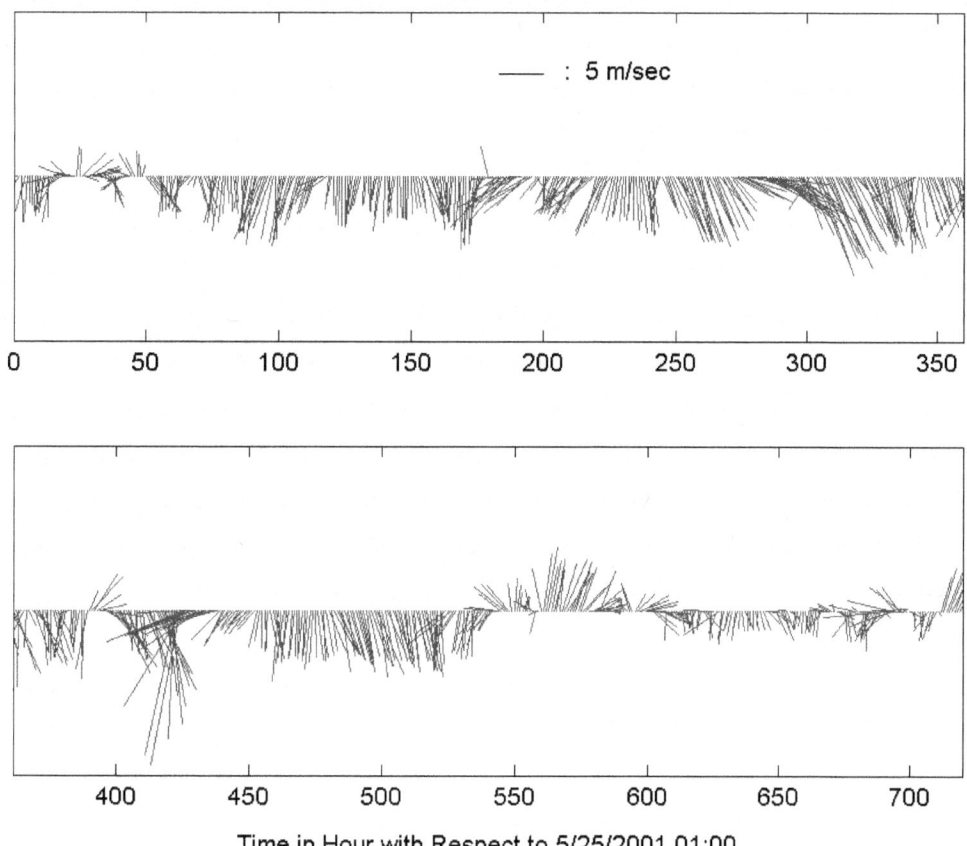

Figure 1-13. Observed wind at GDIL1 for the period 5/25/2001-6/25/2001.

30

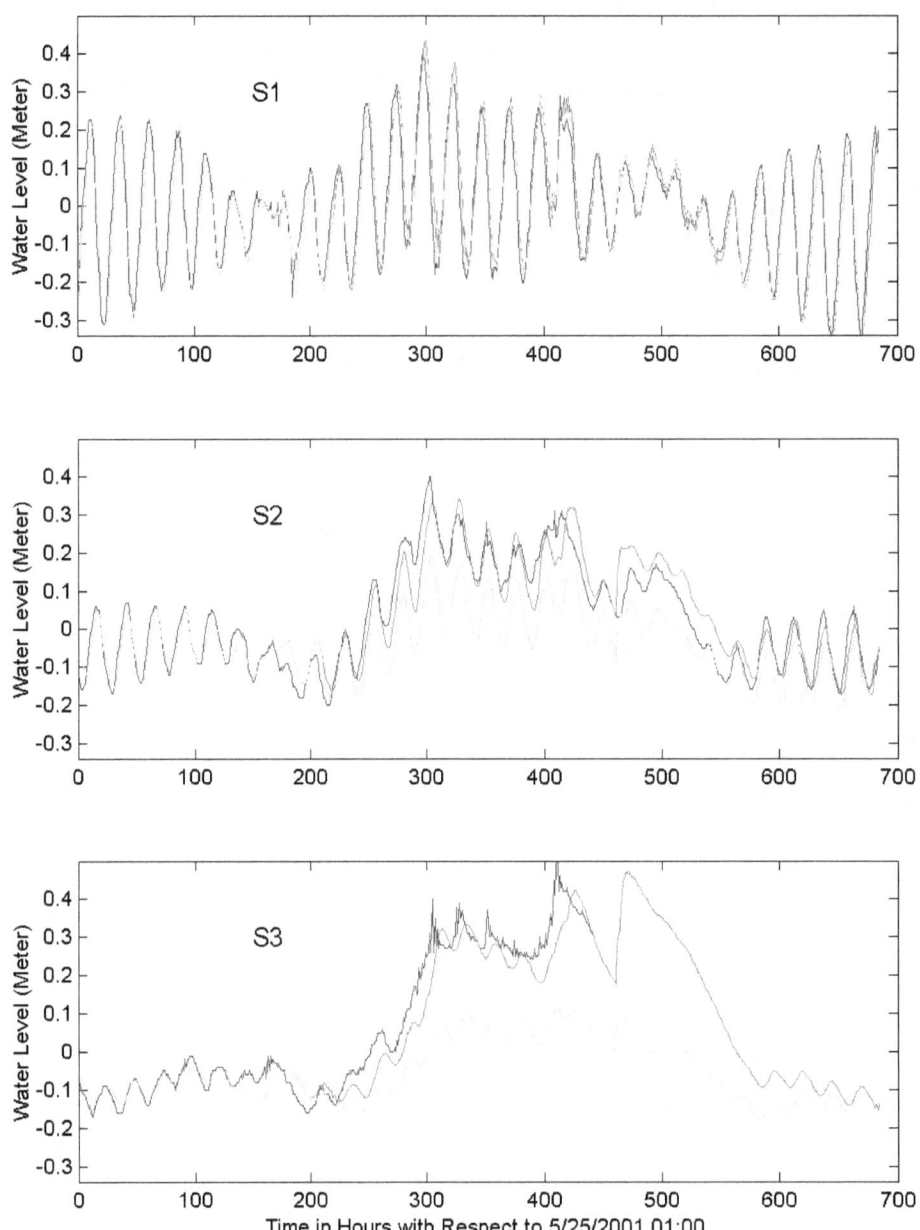

Figure 1-14. Observed (blue) and simulated sea-level heights with (red) and without rainfall (green) at three stations (listed in Figure 1-12) during Allison.

This flood event provided a rare opportunity to test the hydrology model used in this study. The observed rainfall measured at MSY was used to simulate the flood event. In coupling the hydrology model to the hydrodynamic model, it was assumed that 100 % of local rainfall enters the estuary, i.e.; there is no loss of water during the runoff process. This assumption should be reasonable considering the fact that during a heavy rainfall event such as the flood of June 2001; most of the runoff should enter the basin very quickly. Figure 1-13 shows observed and simulateded sea-level heights during the storm. It is apparent that the downstream station (S1) does not exhibit significant impact of the flood. However, the two upstream stations do display significant impact of the flood due to larger land-to-water surface ratio (Figure 1-2). Especially at the uppermost station, S3, runoff due to the flood overwhelms the water level signal after hour 300. Figure 1-14 shows two cases of simulated sea-level heights, one with rainfall and the other without rainfall. It is apparent that rainfall is needed in order to simulate the observed rise in sea-level during the storm. Agreement between the observation and the model simulation with rainfall included is excellent (Figure 1-15), providing confidence for the hydrology model adopted. The observed agreement also provides a justification for adopting 100% coupling between the hydrologic model and hydrodynamic model, at least for this flood event. However, it is expected that during smaller rainfall events coupling should be less than 100%.

1.7 Summary and Conclusions

A high-resolution (with a model grid resolution of 100 m for the hydrodynamic model), integrated hydrology-hydrodynamic model of the Barataria Basin has been developed to simulate the local hydrological cycle over the surrounding drainage basin and hydrodynamics within the basin. In order to explicit account for runoff from the surrounding drainage basin, 64 known streams and 522 unknown streams were identified. Each stream is assigned its own drainage subbasin and each drainage subbasin is classified into one of the eight drainage types with its distinct persistence time. Runoff characteristic for each subbasin is determined by the shape of the unit hydrograph selected for this basin to mimic typical runoff. Runoff from the hydrology model is fed into the depth-integrated hydrodynamic model via all the streams specified within the model domain. Detailed simulation of runoff from the surrounding drainage basins has never been done previously in the Barataria Basin. The hydrodynamic model (Park 2002) is based on the model formulation of Inoue et al. (2001) with much higher grid resolution than the one used by Park (1998) (also see Inoue et al. (1998)).

The integrated model is forced by observed tides coming from the Gulf of Mexico, local wind, rainfall and evaporation over the model domain, salinity and temperature estimated at the open boundary located offshore of the mouth of the bay. Estimated local precipitation and evaporation over the model domain based on actual meteorological observations provide hydrological forcing to the hydrological model, that in turn simulates local runoff into the hydrodynamic model. A novel feature of the hydrodynamic model is its use of a very accurate advection scheme, thus, enabling accurate simulation of salinity variations in response to changes in various hydrological forcing functions. A flood event that took place during the tropical storm Allison in June 2001 resulted in significant sea-level changes especially in the

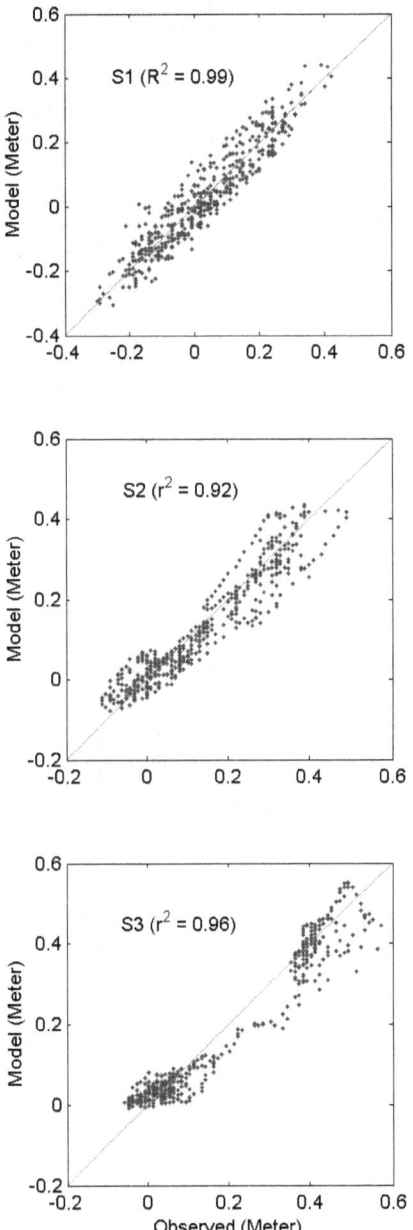

Figure 1-15. Cross correlations between observed and simulated sea-level heights with
rainfall at three stations during Allison.

upstream region of the basin. The integrated model appears to be able to capture a significant portion of the observed sea-level variations during the flood, providing confidence in the integration of the hydrology model and the hydrodynamic model, at least in terms of mass flux between the hydrology and hydrodynamic models. The next step in the model testing and verification is to examine the model's ability to simulate hydrodynamics and salinity distribution within the Barataria Basin. An example of the model simulation is presented in Chapter 2.

CHAPTER 2

MODEL SIMULATION

2.1 Simulation of a Typical Dry Summer Condition

As an example of illustrating the integrated model's ability to simulate hydrodynamics and salinity distribution within the Barataria Basin, a typical dry summer condition was chosen to be simulated. This relatively dry season was selected in order to reduce the noise to signal ratio that might confound the impacts of freshwater diversions. Specifically, using the observed sea level height and salinity estimated at the open boundary, observed wind and precipitation, and estimated evaporation as forcing, model simulation was carried out for a 30-day period from July 7 to August 5, 1999. Figure 2-1 shows the locations of relevant stations. During this period, total precipitation was 6.8 *cm* (Figure 2-2), which is only half of the long-term average of 15 *cm*. Evaporation, however, totaled 11.8 *cm* for the 30 days of the simulation (Figure 2-2).

This simulation period represents typical, environmentally fair, summer conditions of predominantly northerly or southerly breezes of 3 to 7 $m\,s^{-1}$ with occasional shifts in wind direction (Figure 2-3). It should be noted that the wind directions during the first half of the simulation period show primarily southerly breezes except between the 6th and 8th days and that the southerly breezes are still modulated by the land-sea breeze system. During the last 12 days, however, the directions change by day and night due to the temperature differences between land and sea. The most pronounced effect of wind forcing on the Gulf of Mexico systems is the difference between a northerly and a southerly wind (Swenson and Turner, 1998).

In order to delineate relationships between the local wind and water level, approximately four months (4/1/1999-7/30/1999) of hourly records of water level and wind data from GDIL1 were used to estimate the spectral density of water level and wind components. The coherence between water level and wind components was estimated by averaging over 30 frequencies, giving 60 degrees of freedom with a 95% significance level of 0.098 (Figure 2-4). It was found that the coherence between water level and each wind component was frequency dependent. The significant energy peak is at very low frequency, roughly less than 0.01 cph. At short sub-tidal time scales (a few days), the along-estuary wind stress drives an estuarine-shelf exchange; at longer time scales Ekman convergence/divergence driven by alongshore wind stress drives the estuarine-shelf exchange (Schroeder and Wiseman, 1986). Kjerfve (1975), based on a summer field study, suggested that Louisiana estuaries exchange water with the shelf on time scales greater than 1 day in response to Ekman convergence at the coastline driven by the alongshore wind stress.

Salinity studies in coastal areas, including estuaries, are common because of the variability of salinity distribution and its effects upon biota and flow regimes (Byrne et al., 1976). The salinities in Barataria Basin are controlled by rainfall, evaporation, diversions from the Mississippi River, and Mississippi River discharges, and seasonal changes in tide (Barrett, 1971). Until two diversion sites at Naomi and West Pointe à la Hache were constructed, the

36

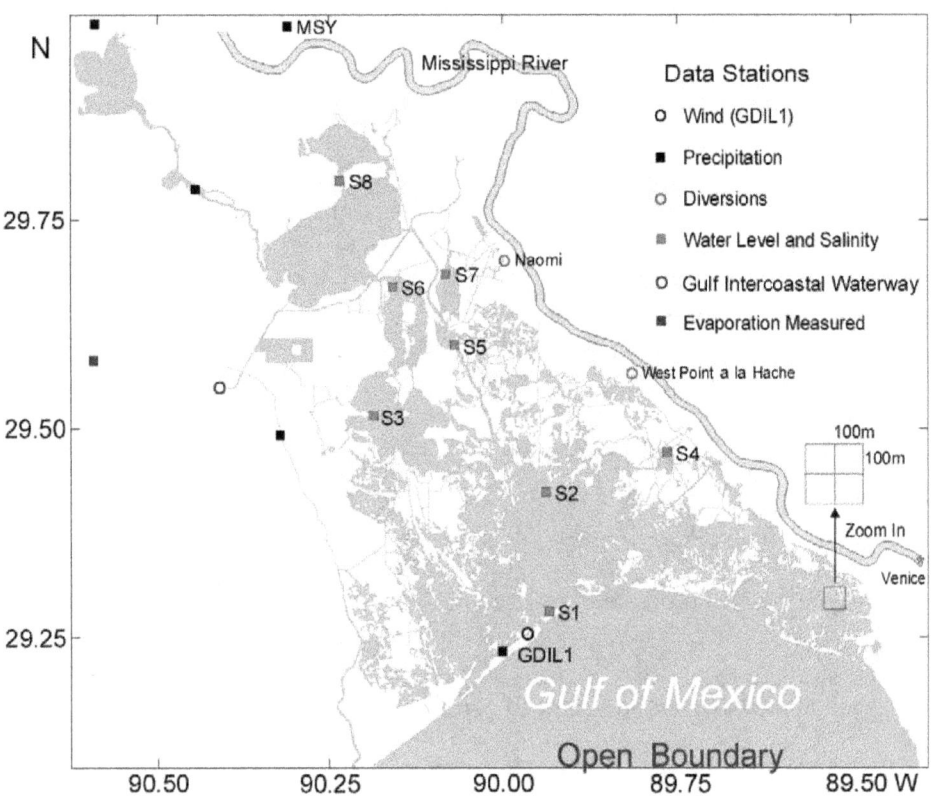

Figure 2-1. Data stations used in model simulation for the simulation period
July 7, 1999 – August 5, 1999.

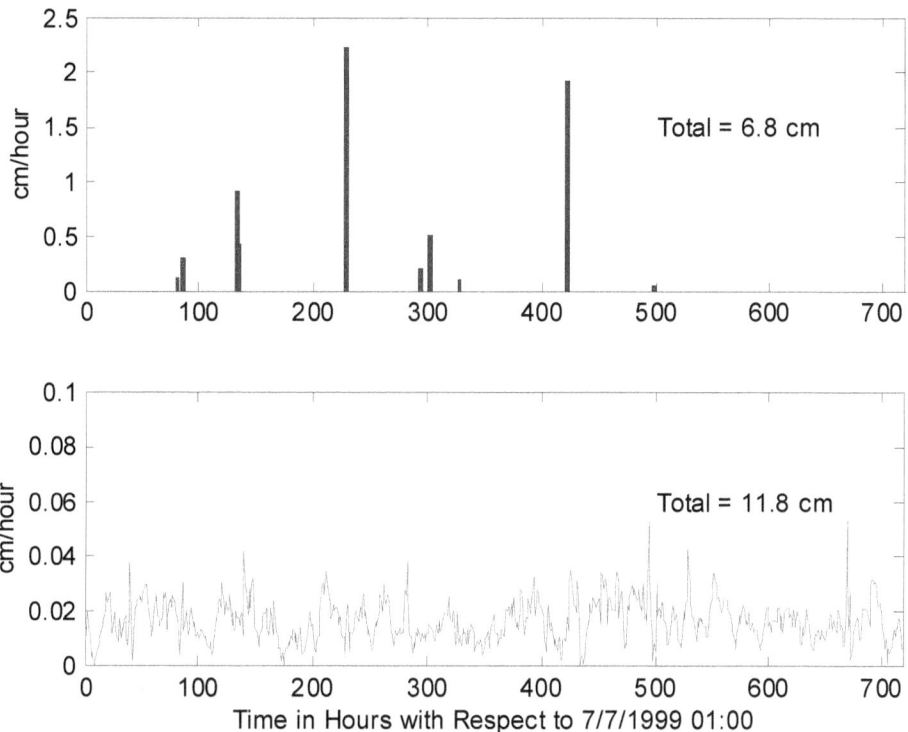

Figure 2-2. Measured precipitation at MSY (upper) and estimated evaporation (lower)
using meteorological observations at GDIL1.

38

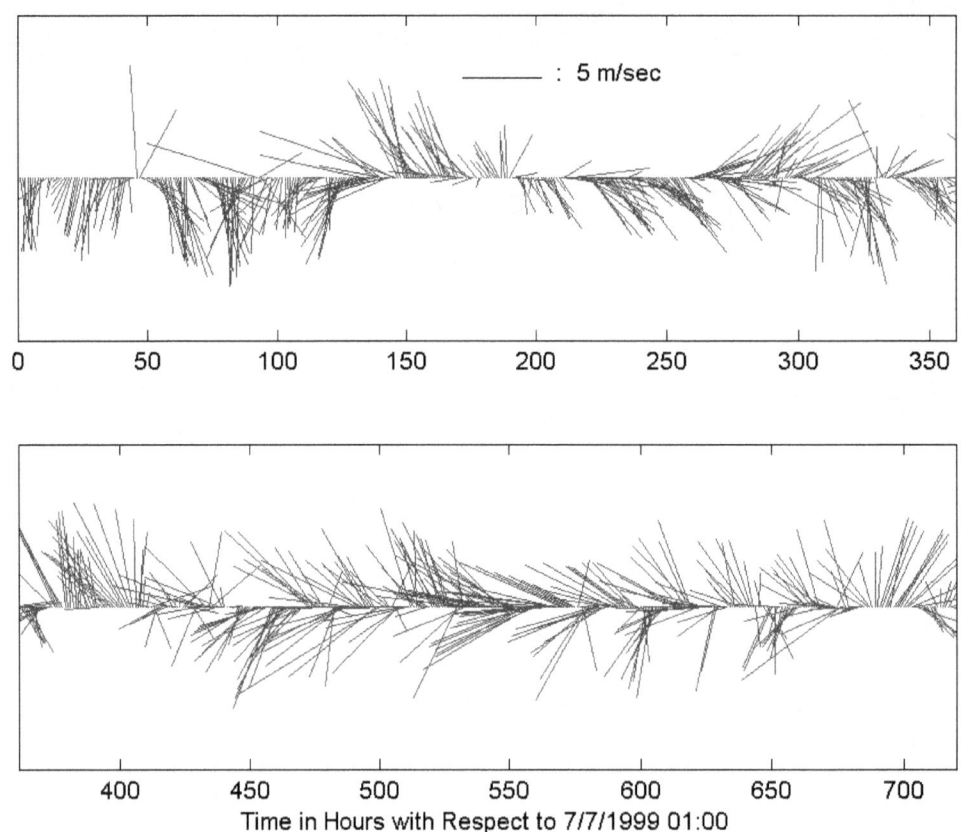

Figure 2-3. Observed wind at GDIL1 for the period 7/7/1999 – 8/5/1999.

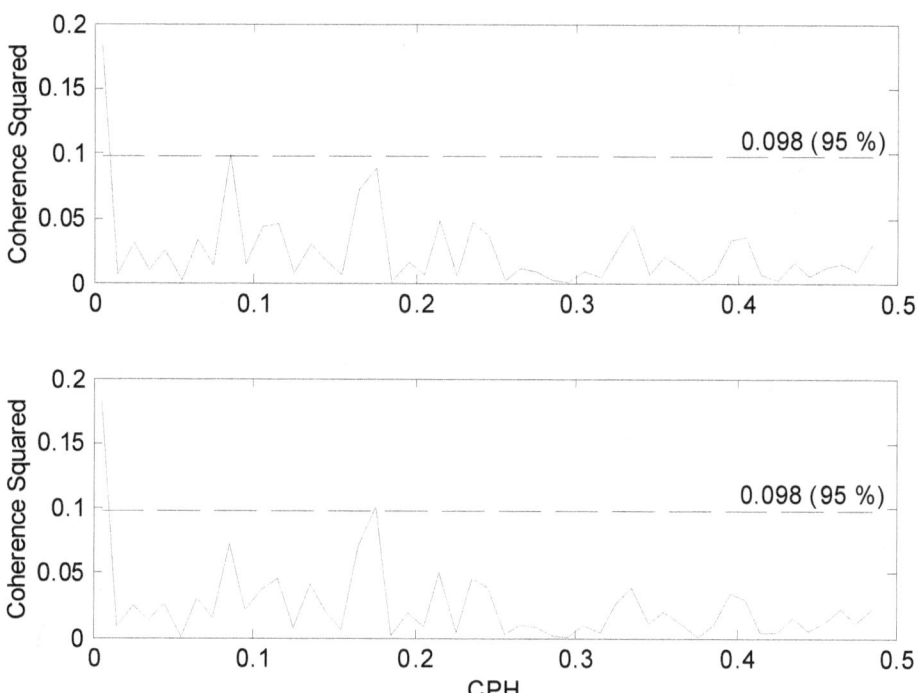

Figure 2-4. Coherence squared between water level at S1 and wind component
at GDIL1 for the period April 1, 1999 – July 30, 1999; eastward stress
(upper) and northward stress (lower).

rainfall was found to be the most dominant contributor in the upper basin. The Mississippi River discharge coming out of the Mississippi Delta located just east of the region is also an important freshwater source in the lower basin. This is obvious in the inverse relationship between Mississippi River discharge and Barataria Basin salinity (Figure 2-5). In order to determine the relationship between salinities in Barataria Basin and Mississippi River discharge, the phase difference was estimated using the Mississippi River water level data at Venice, a surrogate for discharge, and salinities at S1 (Figure 2-5). The regression result shows that there is almost a 13-day phase difference between the two sites.

The initial condition for salinity (Figure 2-6) was estimated based on actual salinity observations at the eight stations (S1 through S8 shown in Figure 2-1) at Hour 0 on July 7, 1999. It should be noted that due to the limited number of observed values used in deriving the salinity initial condition, any salinity signal not captured by the eight stations was not accounted for in the initial condition used. Using the estimated sea level height and salinity at the open boundary based on the observed values at S1, observed precipitation at MSY, and estimated evaporation based on meteorological observations at GDIL1, the model was spun up from rest at 0 hour on July 7, 1999, and the first 5-day period was considered as the spin-up period. During this simulation period actual freshwater diversion rates from the two diversion sites, Naomi and West Pointe à la Hache, varied with time while averaging $14.6\, m^3\, s^{-1}$ and $10.8\, m^3\, s^{-1}$, respectively (Figure 2-7). However, for this model simulation the pumping rates were fixed at zero. Therefore, the model simulation is expected to produce slightly different results from observations. In addition, the freshwater input from the Gulf Intracoastal Waterway was set to $50\, m^3 s^{-1}$, a value close to the long-term mean observed (Swarzenski, personal communication, 2002). The diffusivity was fixed at $5\ m^2\ s^{-1}$.

2.2 Simulation of Water Levels

In order to analyze tidal propagation, a series of 3-hour interval data was extracted from the 30 days of recorded simulation results. The water level on the 501st hour at S1 was selected as a beginning frame for the tidal cycle, slack before flood (Figure 2-8). Figures 2-9a and 2-9b show salinity distribution at 3-hour intervals starting at Hour 501. Barataria Basin is morphologically separated from the Gulf of Mexico by the several islands that block tidal energy from propagating into the bay. Figures 2-9a and 2-9b suggest that the tidal regime within the basin can be divided into four different regions: (1) the Gulf of Mexico, (2) Barataria Bay and Caminada Bay regions, (3) Little Lake and Barataria Waterway regions, and (4) the upper basin regions of Lac des Allemands and Lake Salvador. The separations are characterized by a chain of islands, narrow canals and bayous, and the Gulf Intracoastal Waterway. During the period shown in Figures 2-9a and 2-9b, the tidal range is roughly 40 cm near the mouth of the bay. The tidal amplitudes decrease as tides propagate into the upstream regions. There are some discontinuities at the transitions between Barataria Bay and Barataria Waterway, Little

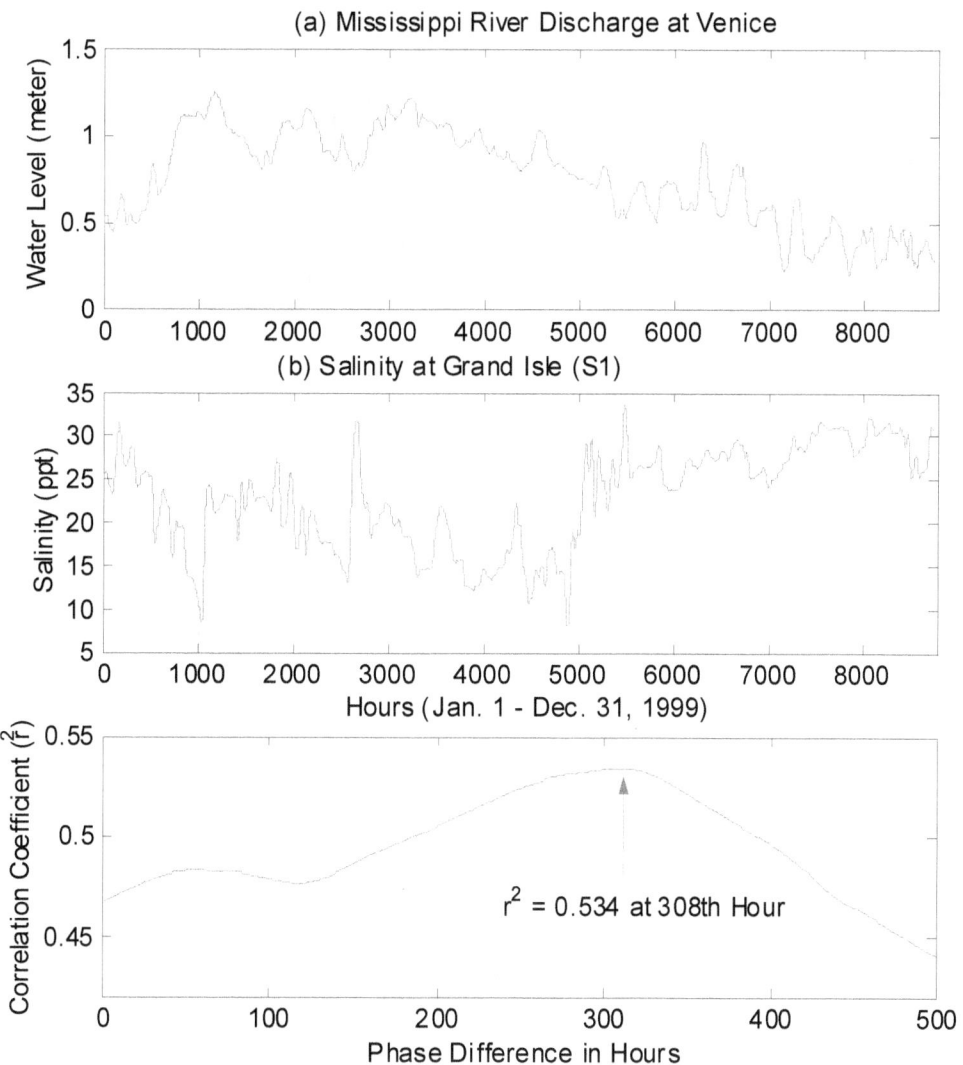

Figure 2-5. Mississippi River stage at Venice (top) and salinity variation
in S1 (Grand Isle) (middle), and their cross-correlation function (bottom).

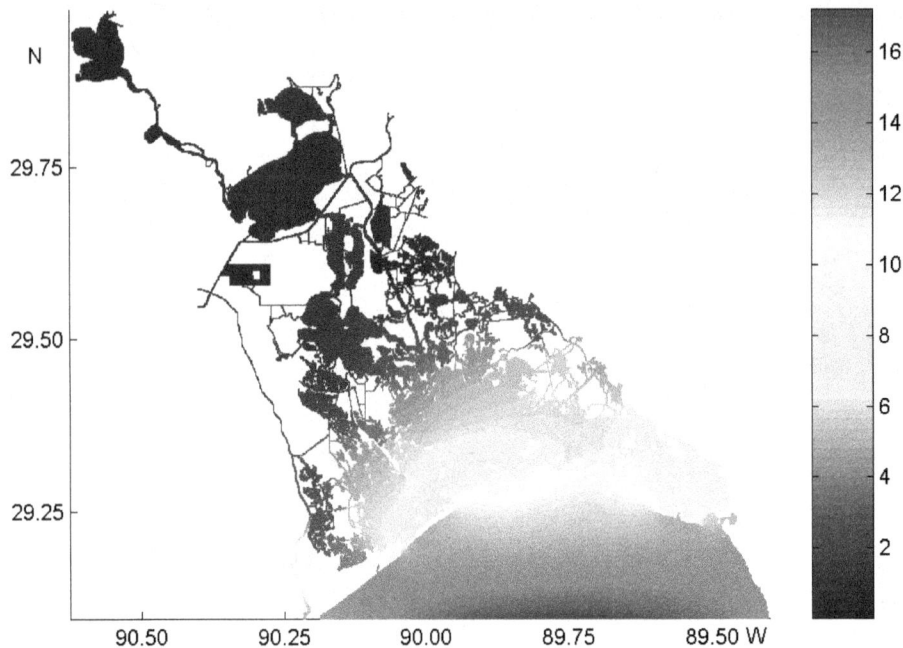

Figure 2-6. Salinity distribution used as initial condition for a typical dry summer
simulation for the period 7/7/1999-8/5/1999. It is based on salinity
observations at eight sites (S1 – S8 shown in Figure 2-1) at 0 Hour on
7/7/1999.

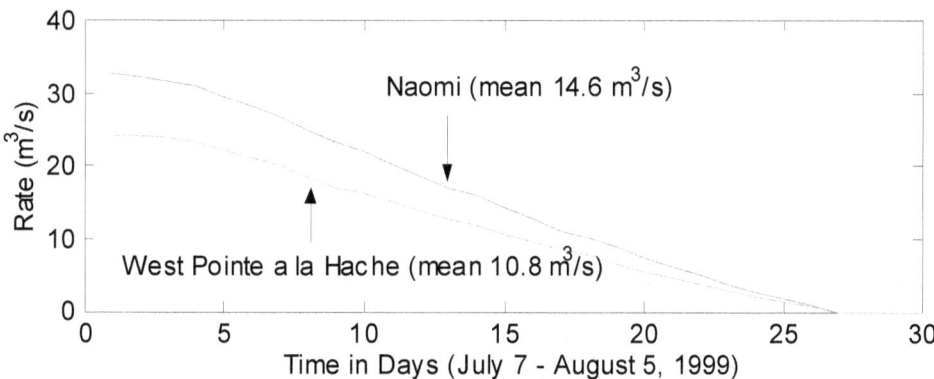

Figure 2-7. Freshwater diversion records at Naomi and West Pointe a la Hache during the simulation period.

44

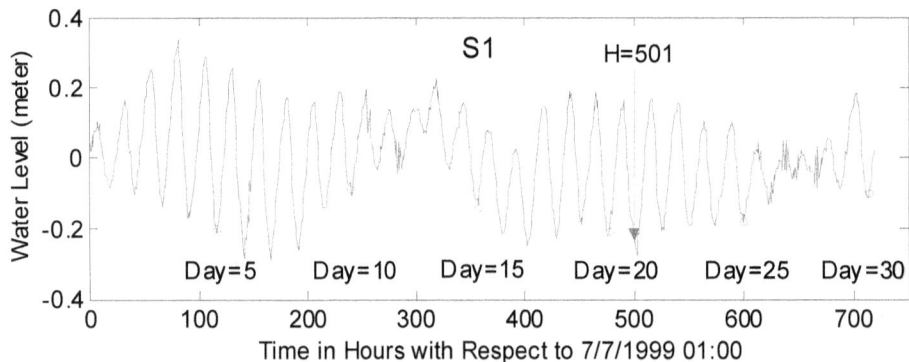

Figure 2-8. Simulated water level at S1. Hour 501 is indicated.

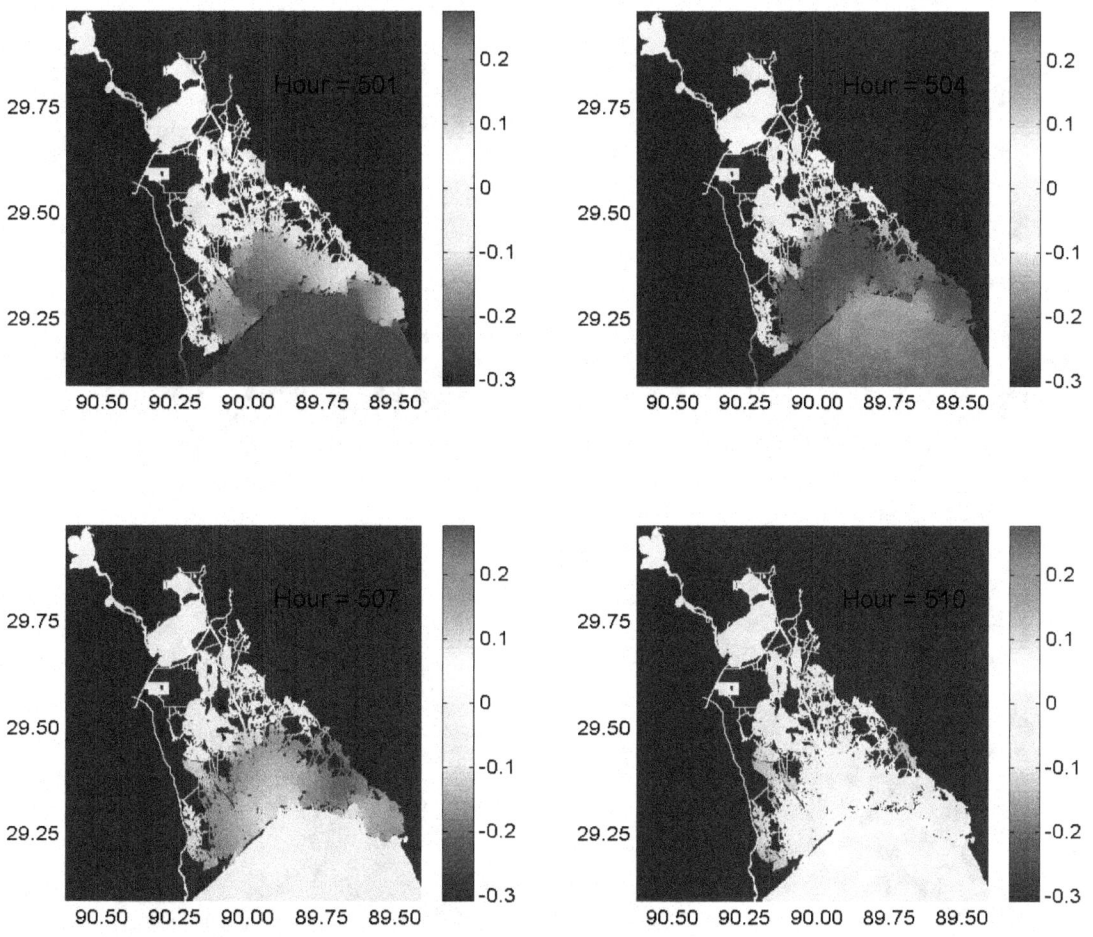

Figure 2-9a. Simulated water level (*m*) at 3-hour intervals for the period Hour 501 – Hour 510.

46

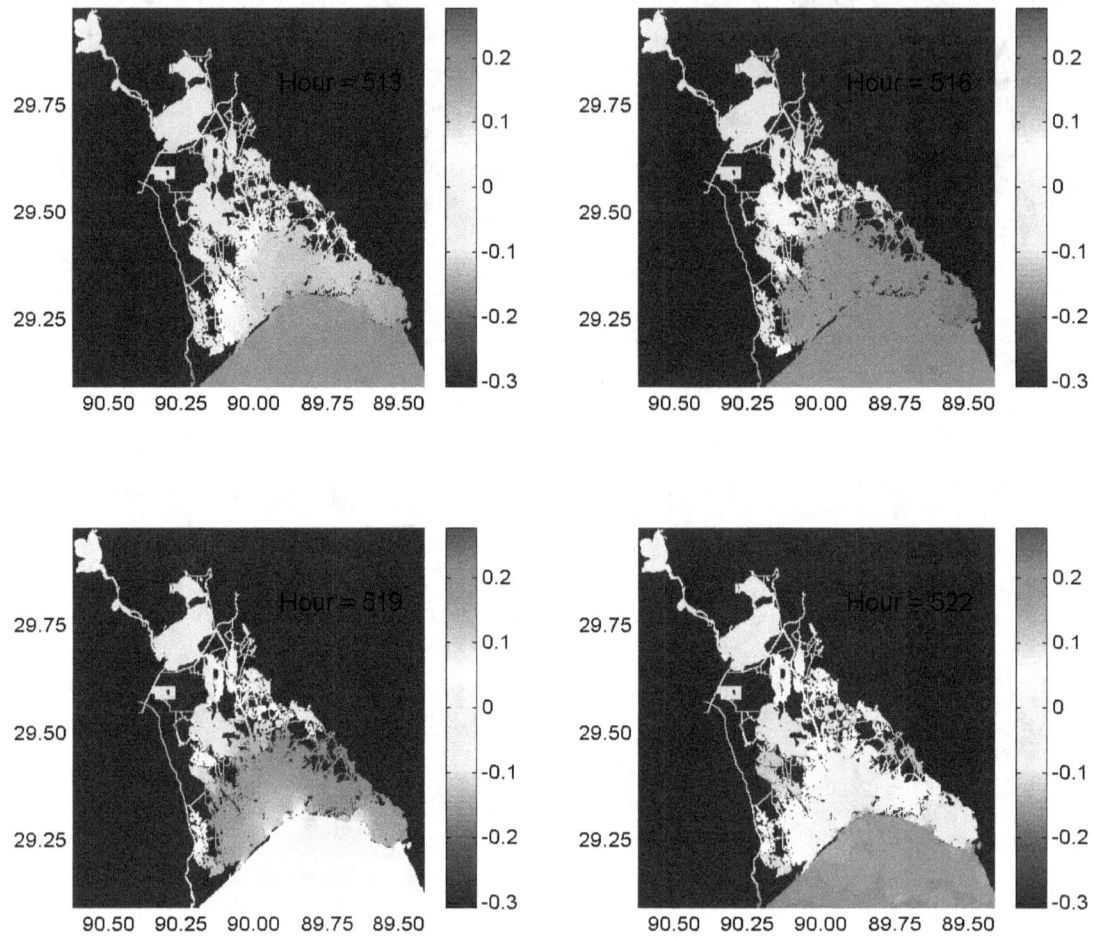

Figure 2-9b. Simulated water level (*m*) at 3-hour intervals for the period Hour 513 – Hour 522.

Lake, and Lake Salvador. It is difficult to distinguish water level changes at upstream sites during a tidal cycle due to the smaller tidal range there compared to that in Barataria Bay and the Gulf of Mexico. Sometimes wind forcing overwhelms astronomical tidal in the shallow regions. The high sea level at hour 501 in the northern lakes is due to the consistent southwesterly wind (Figure 2-3).

Figure 2-10 shows 30 locations selected from the mouth of the bay all the way to the top of the basin (AB) and 20 locations selected from the mouth of the bay to the top of the Barataria Waterway (AC). Figure 2-11 shows water level changes during a tidal cycle, beginning at hour 501, for the locations indicated AB (upper) and AC (lower) in figure 2-10. It is clearly seen that this basin is made of four different sub-regions as discussed previously. Within Barataria Bay, which corresponds to stations 1 through 7, the tidal amplitude is 40-45 *cm*. There is a sudden decrease in amplitude between stations 7 and 9 along transect AB, which lies in the narrow channels between Barataria Basin and Little Lake. Between stations 9 and 12 (Little Lake), the water level changes about 20 *cm* during a tidal cycle. Between stations 12 and 14, there is a sudden decrease across the narrow shoal between Little Lake and Bayou Perot. Near station 15, the water level varies roughly 10 *cm* during a tidal cycle. As the transect enters a narrow region across the Gulf Intracoastal Waterway and proceeds into Lake Salvador, there is a short sudden decrease in amplitude at station 17. Above Lake Salvador, the water level changes during a tidal cycle are about 7 *cm*, and then they smoothly decrease into Lac des Allemands. Along the transect AC there are similar patterns to those observed in Barataria Bay (between stations 1 and 7). Between stations 7 and 8, there is a sudden decrease due to the narrowness of the Barataria Waterway. Beyond station 8, they smoothly decrease to the top of the Barataria Waterway with a small sudden decrease near station 15. It is clearly seen that the water level piled up at hour 501 and 502 in the top of the Barataria Waterway due to the consistent southwesterly wind.

It is interesting to estimate tidal propagation speed throughout the basin. One can simply apply the well-known shallow wave formula, $C = \sqrt{gH}$ as long as the water depth is known. Even though the water depth is known, though, it varies with location. Another method to estimate tidal propagation speed is by applying the Hovmüller diagram, which is a plot of wave amplitude or phase against time and distance. In order to estimate the tidal phase speed for the basin, the thirty stations from Figure 2-10 were used. The tidal amplitudes are plotted against station and time (Figure 2-12). The blue arrow originating at station 1 near hour 81 indicates the propagation of a tidal wave crest and suggests that it takes 16 hours to traverse the system. It is easily seen that some sudden changes in phase velocity appear to occur due to the basin's morphological characteristics. For instance, there is a sudden change near station 17, possibly due to the Gulf Intracoastal Waterway. Tidal propagation speed estimated from the blue arrow in Figure 2-12 is 1.94 m s^{-1}, that can be compared to the speed of ~ 3.83 m s^{-1} based on the shallow-water wave formula with H=1.5 m, suggesting that it is often difficult to estimate actual tidal propagation speed by the simple shallow-water wave formula.

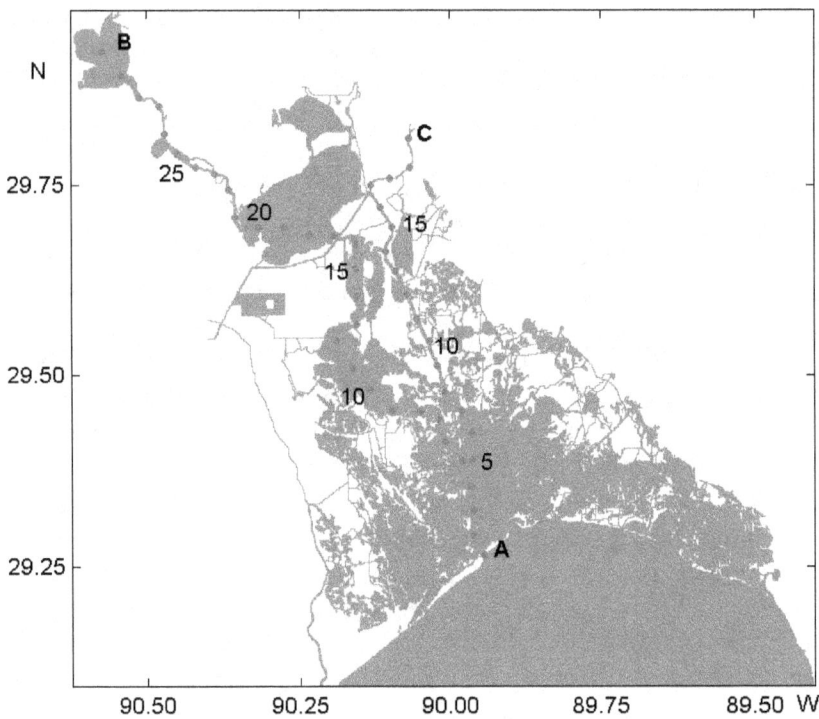

Figure 2-10. Selected locations from the mouth of the bay to the uppermost reaches of the basin (AB) and to the top of the Barataria Waterway (AC).

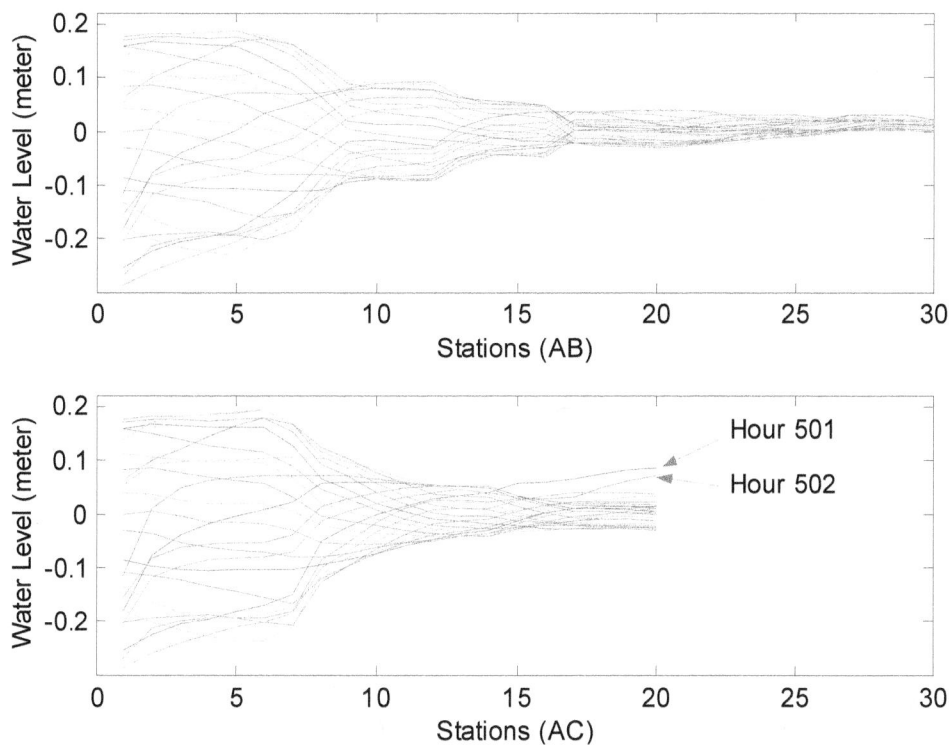

Figure 2-11. Simulated water level changes during a tidal cycle starting at Hour 501 at locations indicated AB (upper) and AC (lower) in Figure 2-10. Barataria Bay and Caminada Bay regions extend from Stations 1 to 7 for both AB and AC. Little Lake and Barataria Waterway regions extend from Stations 7 to 16 for AB and from Stations 7 to 20 for AC. The upper basin regions of Lac des Allemands and Lake Salvador extend from Stations 16 to 30 for AB.

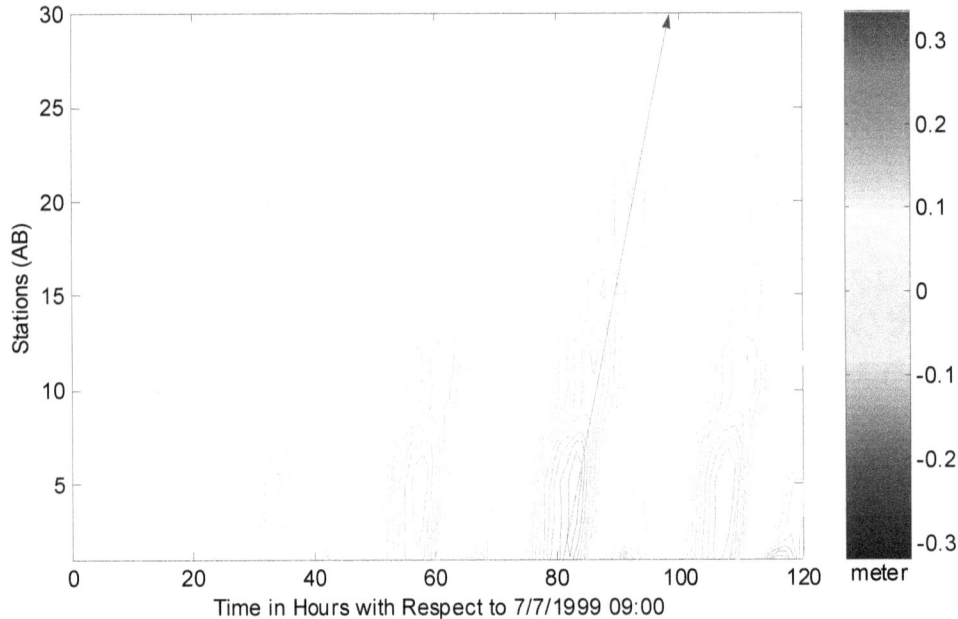

Figure 2-12. Hovmüller diagram: water level vs. time and station location.
Blue arrow estimates a characteristic of tidal propagation.

2.3 Simulation of Salinity

In order to analyze the horizontal salinity variability during the simulation period, a series of data, sampled at 5-day intervals was extracted (Figures 2-13a through 2-13c). All data periods selected were near the slack before flood in order to remain consistent relative to tidal phase. On day 5, since the stage at the moment of the snapshot was near the beginning of flood for the mouth of Barataria Pass, maximum plume excursion from the mouth of the passes was observed. Inside the bay, lower salinities extended to the mouth of the basin. It can be seen easily that the high salinities are coming from the open boundary. It is notable that there are large gradients in the coastal waters due to the time and space variations of salinity imposed along the open boundary.

On day 10, the situation is similar to that of day 5 except for the higher salinity values coming from the open boundary. By day 25, very high values of salinity are coming from the open boundary and penetrating far into the basin. There are big salinity gradients in the northeast region of the Gulf of Mexico in the model domain. On day 30, after several days of high salinity values at the open boundary, the high gradients increase at the coast.

In shallow, bar-built estuaries, it is often assumed that the flow field is vertically homogeneous (Wiseman, 1996). When the estuary is shallow, the velocity shear on the bottom may be large enough to mix the water column completely and make the estuary vertically homogeneous (Dyer, 1973). The concern over the use of a two-dimensional model for this modeling study is in its application to deep channels, waterways, or passes, such as the Barataria Pass. As mentioned earlier, the Barataria Basin has five passes that connect to the Gulf of Mexico. Except for Barataria Pass, all of the other passes are very shallow. Barataria Pass, however, is wide (about 1 *km*) and deep (deeper than 12 *m* in the middle of the pass) perhaps allowing some stratification to be present, i. e., salt wedge might exist along the bottom during flood tide. This phenomenon can not be accounted for in the model.

Figure 2-14 shows observed and simulated salinity at eight stations. It is apparent that at all the stations simulated salinity can capture low-frequency salinity variability but higher-frequency signal is missed. This is due to the fact that the salinity initial condition was based on salinity observations at the eight stations, and it completely missed any smaller horizontal-scale variability that might have existed at that time. Subsequent tidal advection of the smaller-scale salinity variability cannot be simulated by the model as long as the salinity initial condition does not contain the signal. As far as the low frequency variability is concerned, the model appears to capture large portion of the signal at all the stations. After Day 16, the observed salinity at S1 shows significant increase apparently due to an intrusion of saltier water from the Gulf of Mexico. This salty intrusion propagates upstream reaching S2 after Day 25, and S5 soon after. Presently, the model is not capable of capturing the observed increases in salinity at S1 due to the present model open boundary set-up where its corresponding salty water has to propagate from the open boundary to S1. At station S5, the instrument error resulted in the loss of usable data at

52

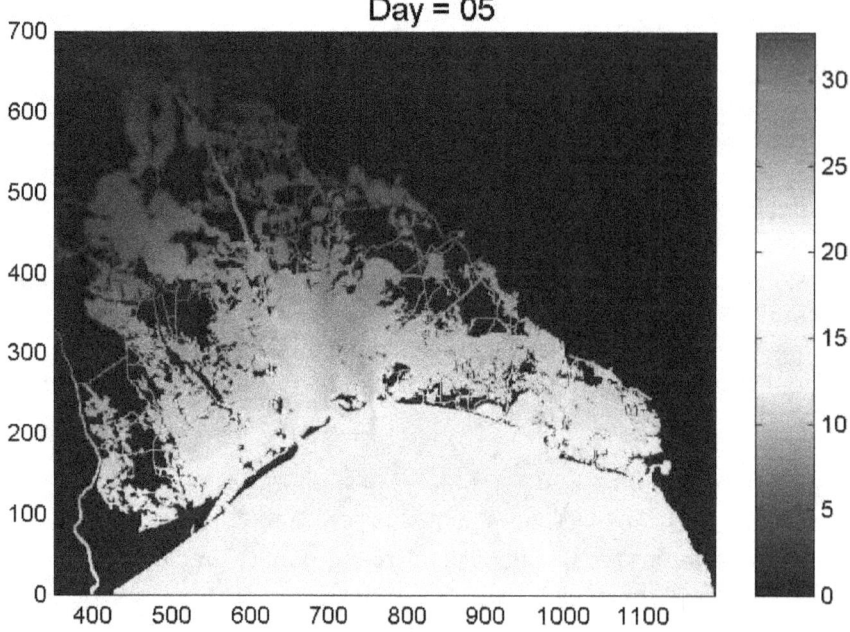

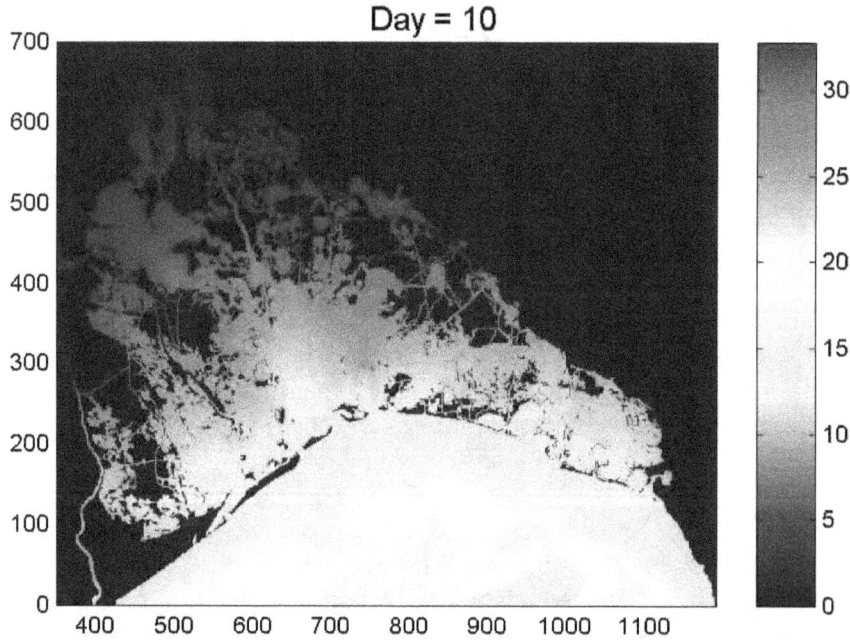

Figure 2-13a. Simulated horizontal salinity (*ppt*) distribution at Day 5
and Day 10 during the simulation period 7/71999 – 8/5/1999.
All time slices selected were near the slack before flood.

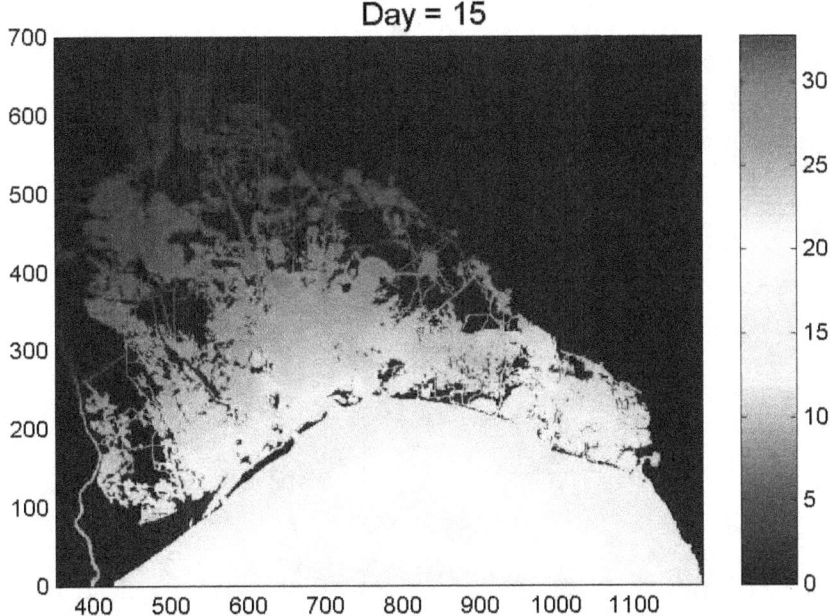

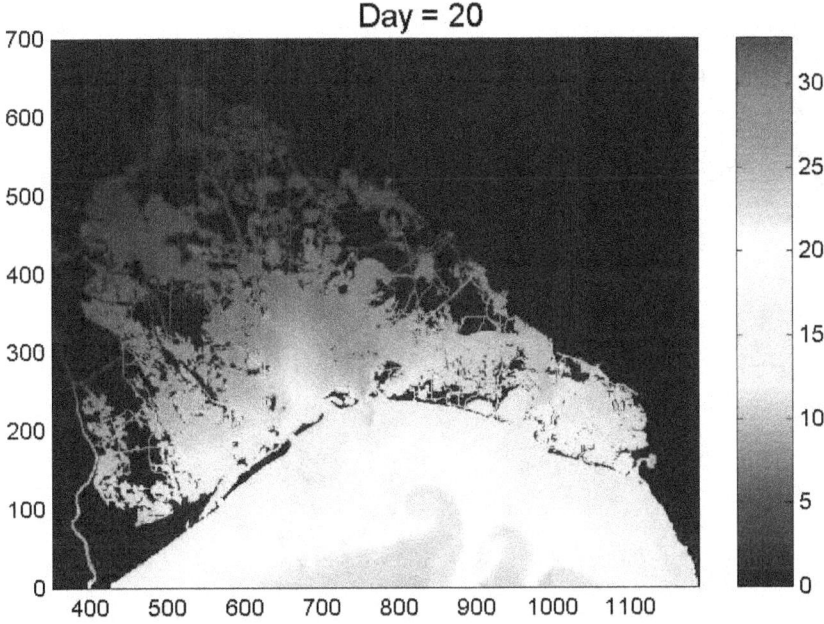

Figure 2-13b. Simulated horizontal salinity (*ppt*) distribution at Day 15
and Day 20 during the simulation period 7/7/1999 – 8/5/1999.
All time slices selected were near the slack before flood.

54

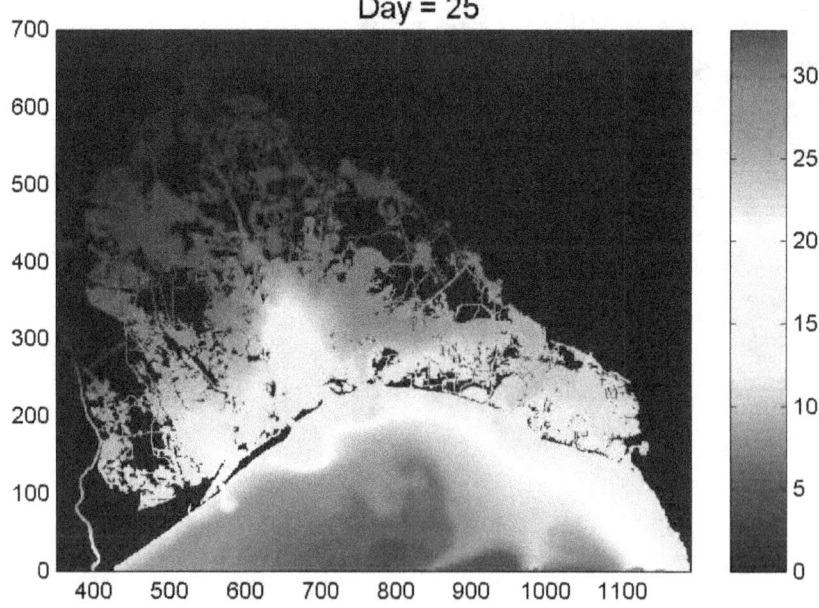

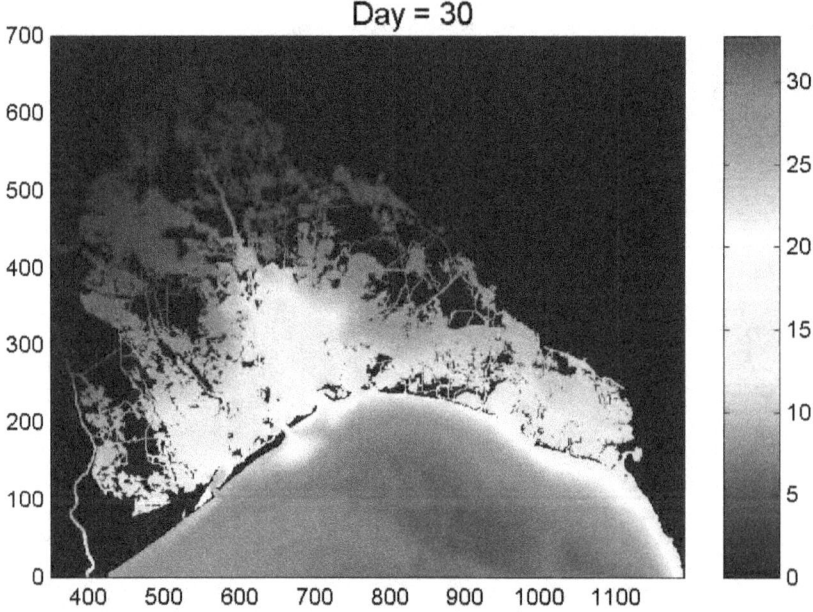

Figure 2-13c. Simulated horizontal salinity (*ppt*) distribution at Day 25
and Day 30 during the simulation period 7/7/1999 – 8/5/1999.
All time slices selected were near the slack before flood.

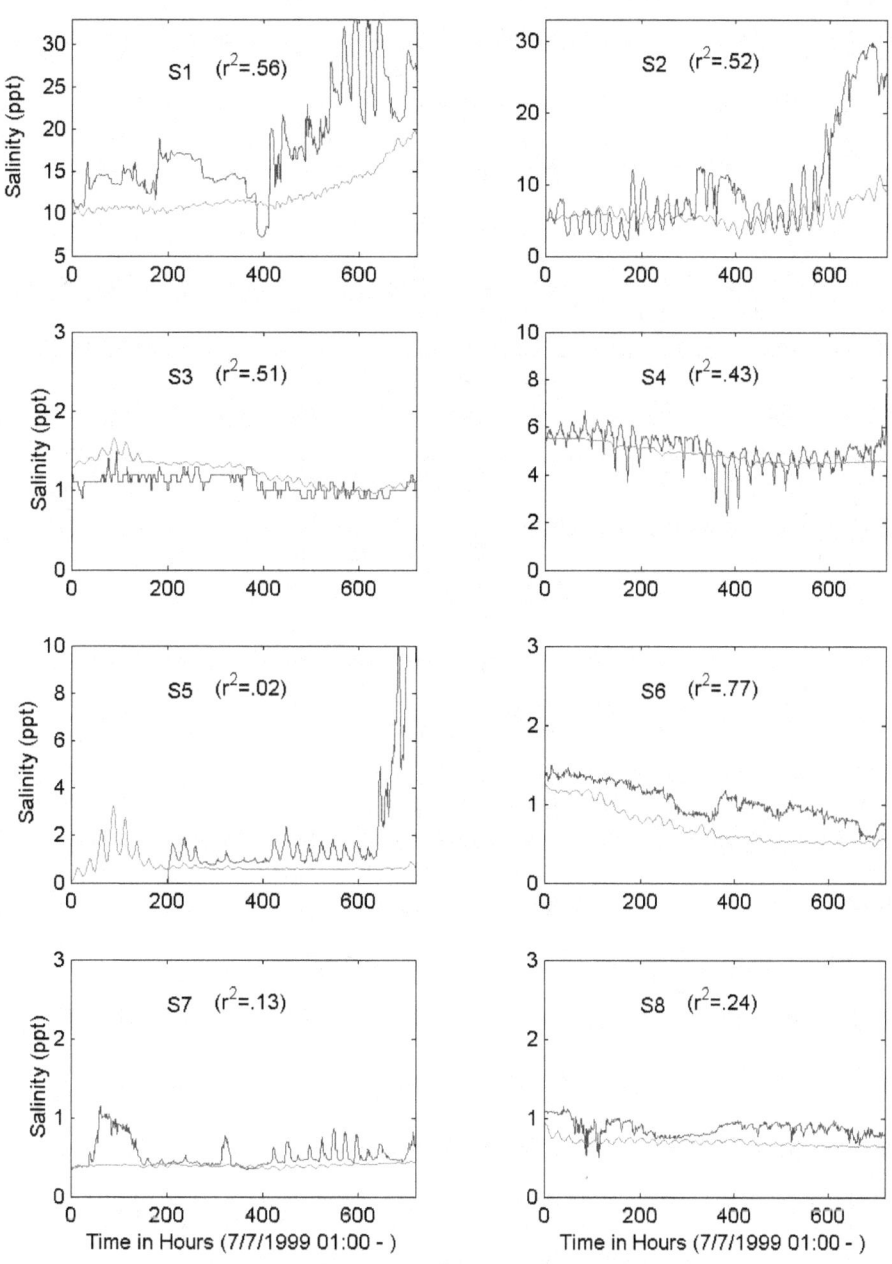

Figure 2-14. Observed (blue) and simulated salinity (red) at eight stations (listed in Figure 2-1).

the beginning of the record until Day 5. At stations further upstream, the overall results look better than those downstream due to the relatively short simulation period that did not allow upstream propagation of the salty intrusion coming from the Gulf of Mexico. One way to improve simulation is to assimilate observed salinity at the mouth of Barataria Pass, thus directly forcing the salinity at the mouth of the bay rather than at the offshore open boundary. Availability of better salinity initial condition with much higher spatial resolution can certainly contribute to improving model simulation. In summary, it is rather encouraging that a 30-day model simulation based on the salinity initial condition estimated from only eight stations can capture bulk of low-frequency signal.

In order to describe tidal mixing of salinity and tidal plume characteristics, a series of 2-hour interval salinity snapshots over a tidal cycle were extracted and zoomed in on at the mouths of the basin (Figures 2-15a and 2-15b). The first snapshot, begins at hour 500, shows slack before flood. Outflow plumes are easily seen at the three passes. During this stage, the plumes reach maximum size. The largest plume, 3 *km* in diameter, extends from Barataria Pass. There are sharp salinity gradients along the frontal zone of the plume. A mushroom-like plume 2 *km* in diameter formed at the mouth of Quatre Bayou Pass. Although the size of the plume is slightly smaller than that from Barataria Pass, the salinity gradient is greater than that at Barataria Pass due to the lower salinity inside the bay. Although the flood has already begun, the scales of plume do not change significantly for the next several hours, while their shapes do change. However, inflow plumes are noticeable inside the bay by hour 506. At hour 508, the plumes from all three passes were clearly retracting into the basin under incoming flood tide and forming well-defined inflow plumes inside the bay. It should be noted that high salinity values are detectable along the left side of Barataria Pass during the flood, probably due to the alongshore salinity gradient immediately offshore. Unlike the outflow plumes, the inflow plumes spread much wider. By hour 512, most of the outflow plumes disappeared. At hour 518, inflow plumes reached their maximum length of 11 *km*. Some of this water remained in the bay over the entire cycle. After hour 520, the inflow plume began to move back out through the passes. In summary, the high resolution of the model allows detailed simulation of exchange and mixing processes near the main passes. It appears that mixing and exchange processes at the passes are very complex partly due to the highly complex morphological characteristics of the bay, and a very high model grid resolution is required in order to correctly simulate mixing and exchange processes at those passes.

2.4 Impact of Diversions at Naomi and West Pointe à la Hache

In order to simulate the impact of two smaller freshwater diversion sites, namely, Naomi and West Pointe à la Hache, their maximum rate ($60 \, m^3 \, s^{-1}$) was used in the second model simulation run for the same period. By adopting the maximum rate, it is
our intention to delineate maximum impact to be expected if those two diversions were operating at their peak capacity.

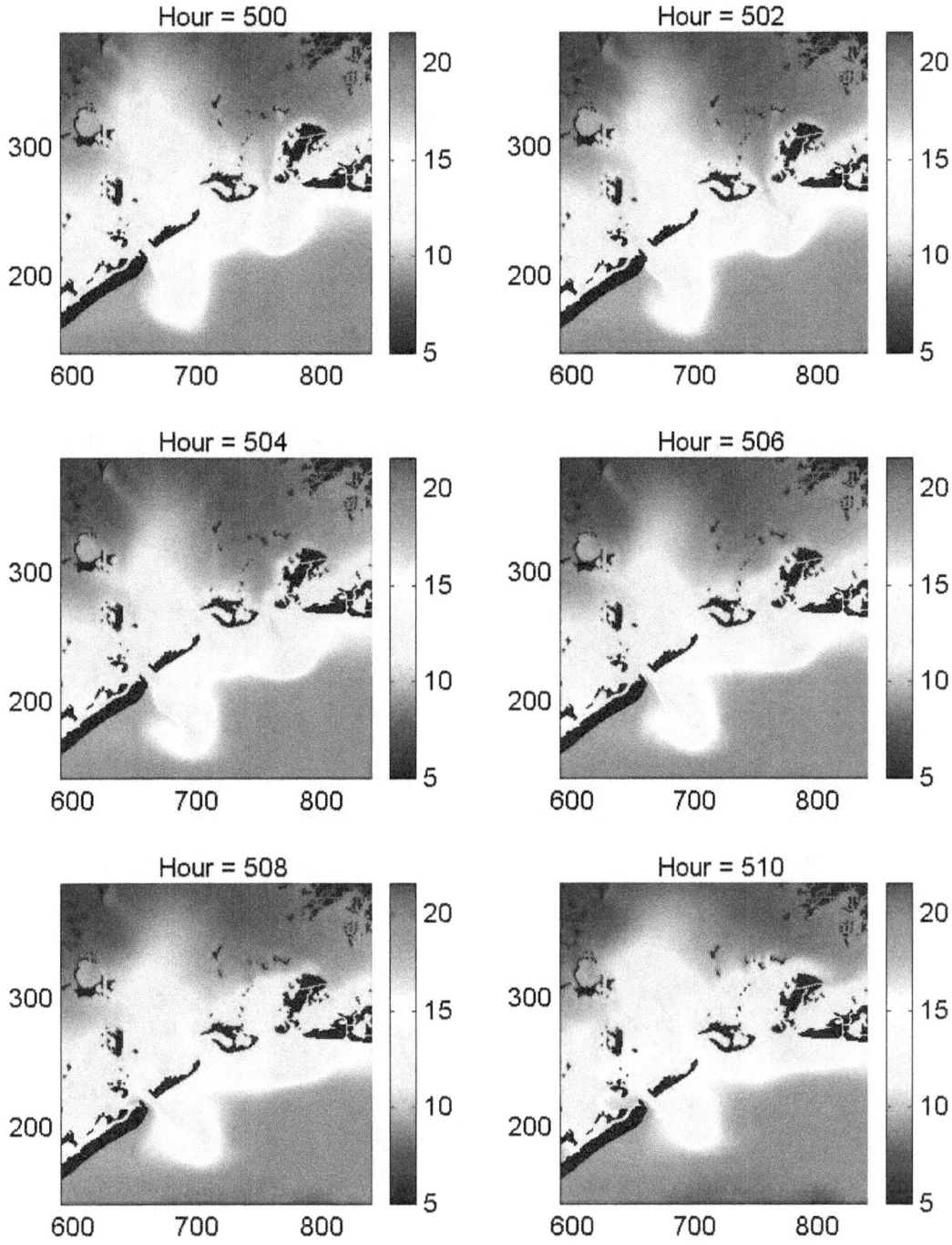

Figure 2-15a. Simulated salinity illustrating inflow and outflow plumes at the mouth
of the Barataria Bay at 2-hour intervals for the period Hour 500 –
Hour 510.

58

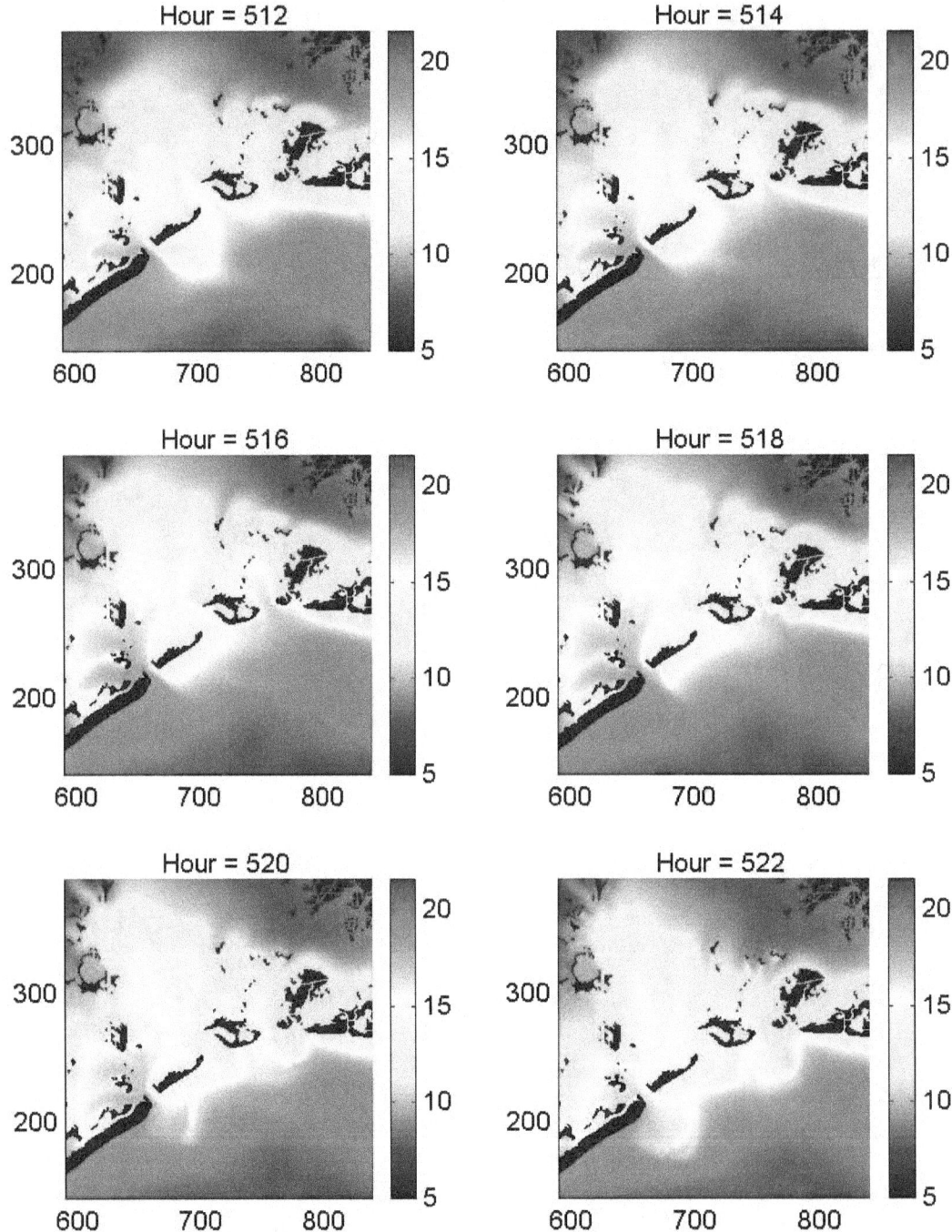

Figure 2-15b. Simulated salinity illustrating inflow and outflow plumes at the mouth of the Barataria Bay at 2-hour intervals for the period Hour 512 – Hour 522.

To characterize the influence of the freshwater diversions from the Mississippi River, the model results with freshwater diversions were subtracted from the results without freshwater diversions. Figure 2-16 shows 5-day interval snapshots colored with the maximum difference set at 6 ppt. On day 10, Barataria Waterway contained a nearly 1.5 ppt difference. When freshwater from West Pointe à la Hache reached Barataria Bay, the impact seemed to accelerate. It is clear that high salinity differences are confined to the vicinity of the diversions. It is roughly estimated that the impact of freshwater diversion reaches the Gulf of Mexico in around 10 to 15 days after the freshwater release. After 15 days, freshwater diversion seemed to impact most of the downstream region of the Barataria Basin except the eastern most part of Barataria Bay and Caminada Bay that appear to be somewhat isolated from the open water of the bay. In the middle of Barataria Bay, the difference reached near 2 ppt. By day 25, most of the downstream basin was measurably impacted by freshwater diversion. Even after day 30, some isolated pockets of unaffected area still remain. It is apparent that in the vicinity of the main passes, impact of diversion is reduced due to the strong tidal mixing.

Figure 2-17 presents horizontal water level differences between the two cases, with and without freshwater diversions, at 4-hour intervals, during the first day of simulation. At hour 4, the signal covered the two neighboring diversion sites and traveled over a region almost 5 *km* in diameter. By hour 8, this signal propagated almost 15 *km* including Lake Salvador. Some signal is detectable coming from the Gulf Intracoastal Waterway. At hour 12, the signal covered nearly the entire middle basin, about 20 *km* in diameter. At hour 20, the signal covered almost the entire basin, except the lower Barataria Bay and Lac des Allemands, with a value bigger than 0.2 *cm*. Figure 2-18 shows the daily water level difference snapshots during the first six days setting the maximum at 1 *cm*. On day 2, the entire basin was under the impact of the diversions except the eastern part of Barataria Bay. Some parts of Caminada Bay seemed to be affected by the Gulf Intracoastal Waterway. On day 3, the signal reached the Gulf of Mexico. On day 4, the water level difference surpassed a value of 1 *cm* in the upper Barataria Basin while the signal in Barataria Bay was rather reduced by the strong tidal dispersion. On day 5, the situation was similar to the previous day, but the downstream region exhibited increased impact due to reduced tidal energy. On day 6, the impact of the freshwater diversion remained relatively unchanged. It is apparent that the water level signal associated with the release of freshwater at the diversion sites propagates at the speed of shallow-water wave, somewhat analogous to tidal bore. Consequently, depth-integrated salinity, which is simulated in the model, will reflect the propagation of water level signal. Those observations suggest that impact of freshwater diversion propagates at speeds much faster than diffusion time scale suggested for mixing of two different water masses often considered for estuaries (e. g., Elliot and Reid, 1976).

Figure 2-19 shows water level difference snapshots every 5 day. On day 10, in the upstream, differences seemed to decrease compared to the previous days probably due to the draining of the initial pile-up of water. On day 20, the differences were largest of all during the 30 days. The maximum water level difference between the two cases is 18 *cm* near the Naomi diversion around day 20. In actual situation, because there are numerous connections between open waters and the diversions, which are not resolved by our present model grid of 100 m, these

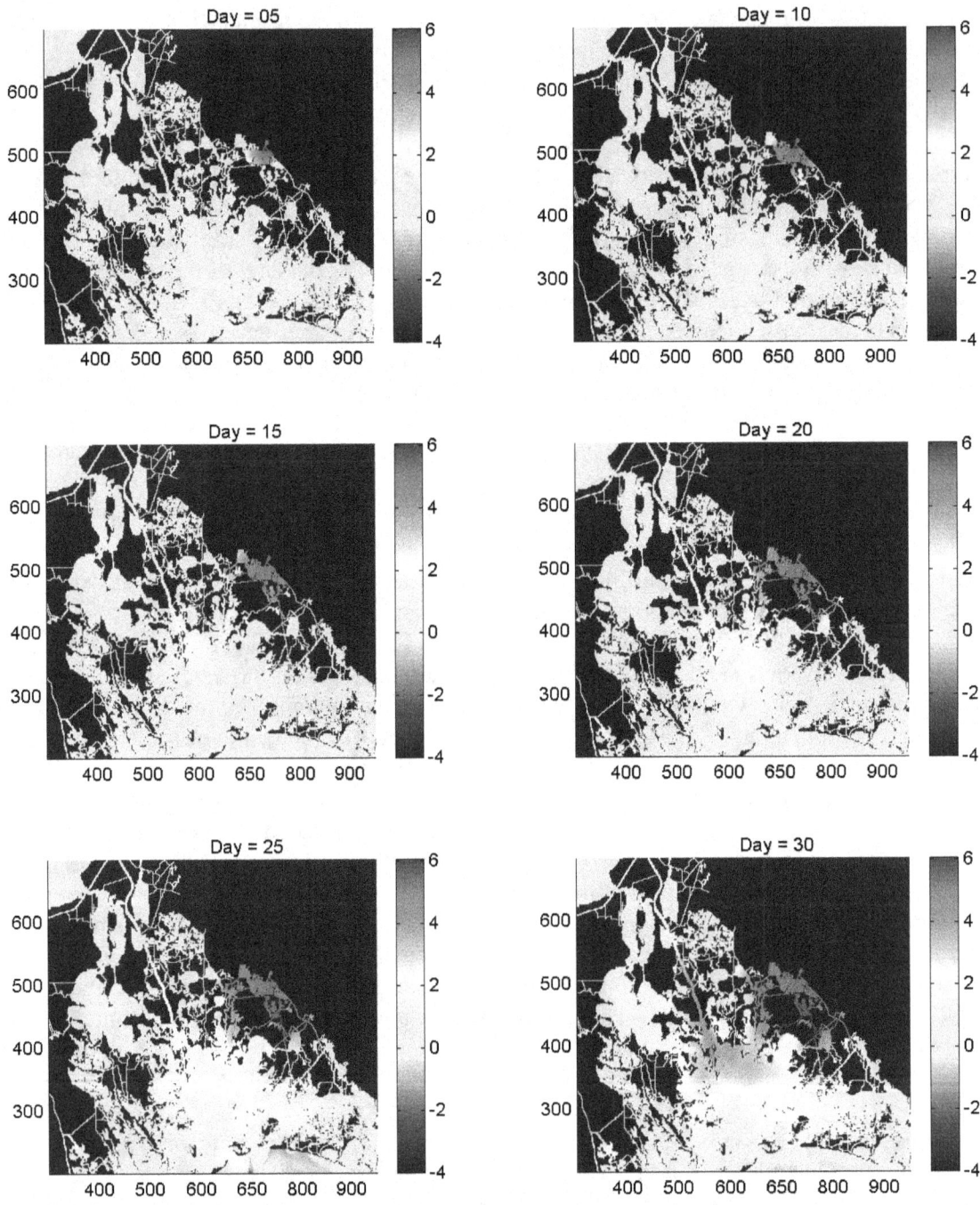

Figure 2-16. Simulated salinity differences (*ppt*) between without and with freshwater diversions (without – with) at Naomi and West Pointe à la Hache at 5-day intervals.

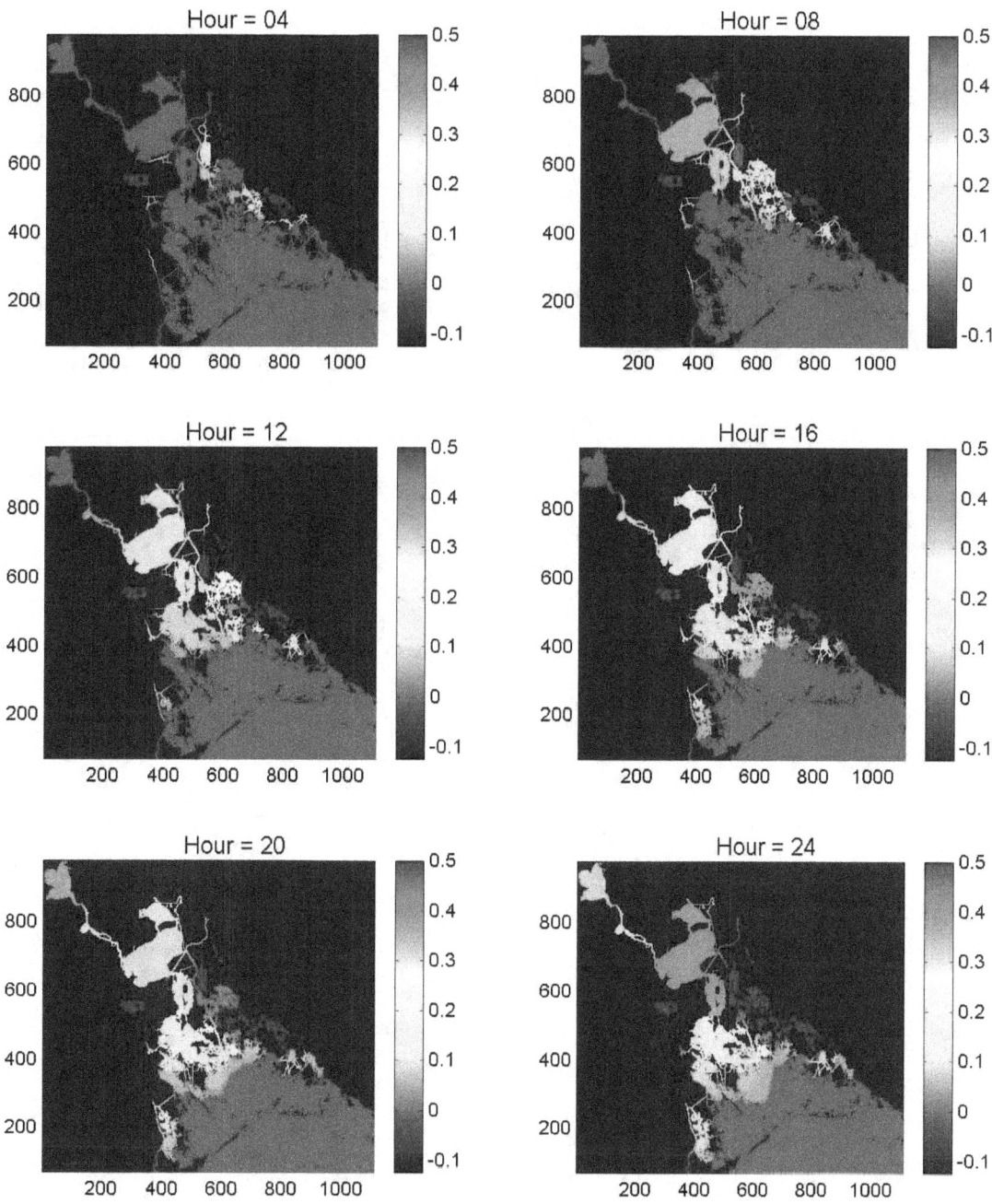

Figure 2-17. Simulated water level differences (*cm*) between with and without freshwater diversions (with – without) at Naomi and West Pointe à la Hache during the first day of simulation.

62

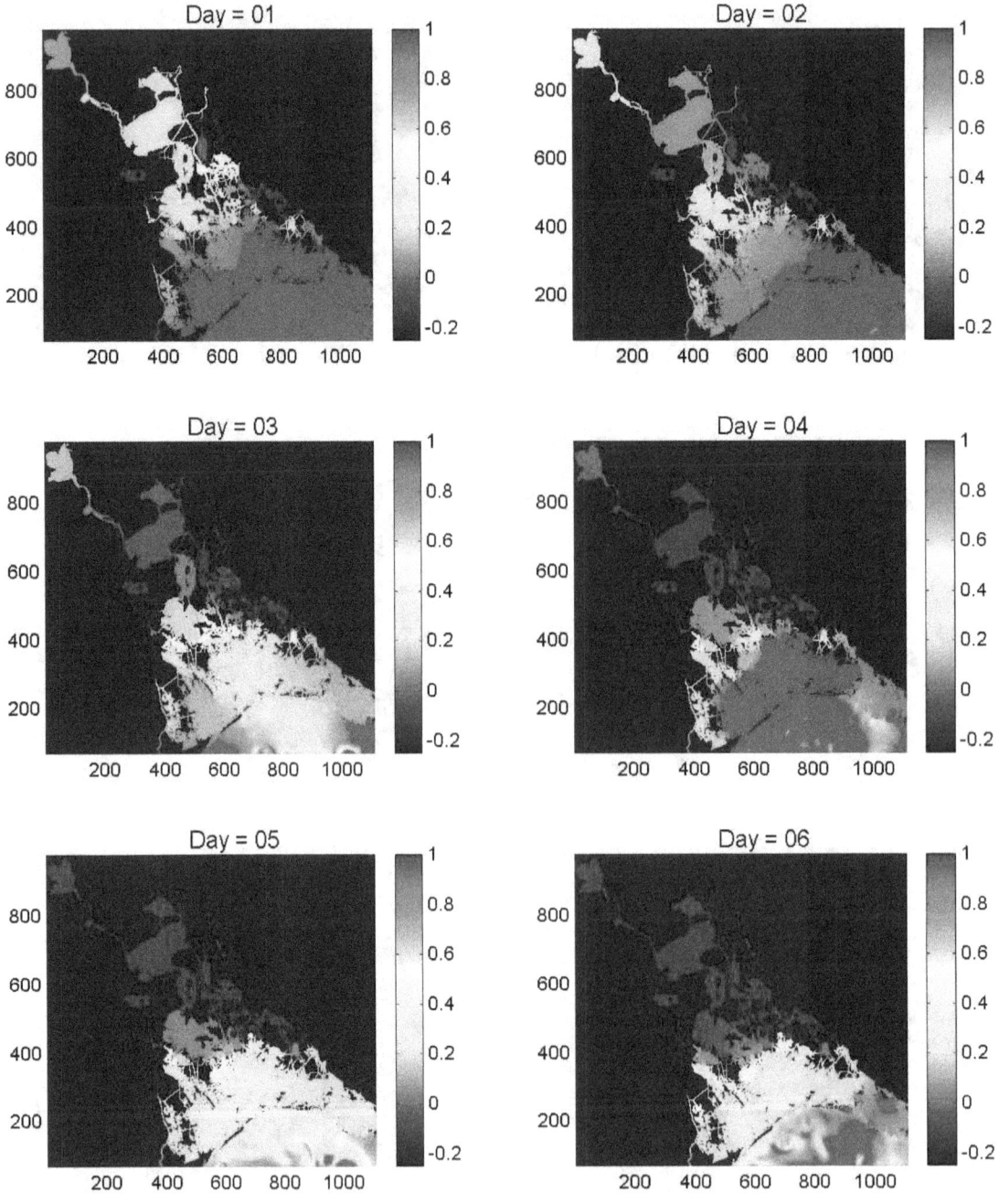

Figure 2-18. Simulated water level differences between (*cm*) with and without
freshwater diversions (with – without) at Naomi and West Pointe à la
Hache during the first six days of simulation.

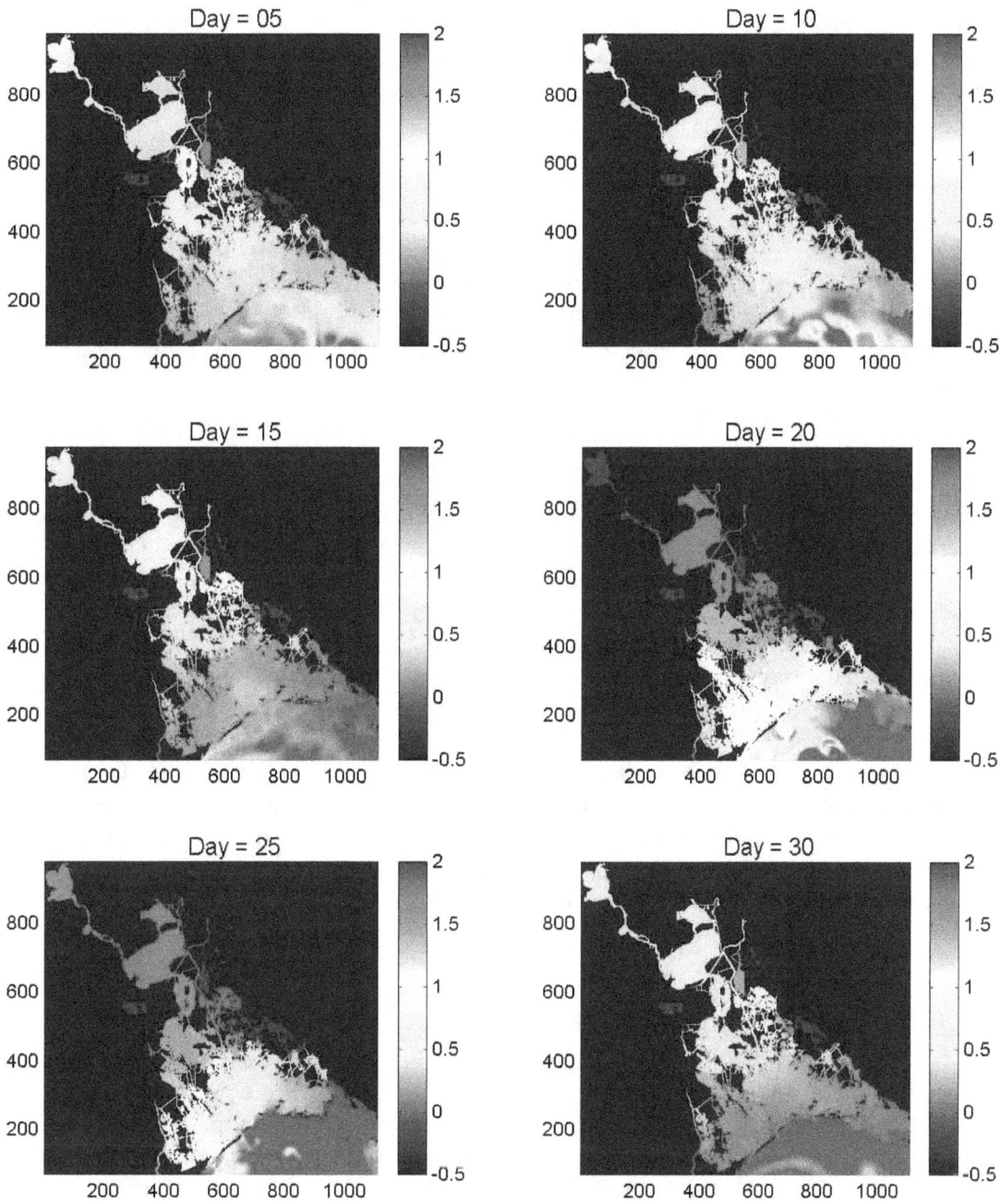

Figure 2-19. Simulated water level differences (cm) at 5-day intervals between with and without freshwater diversions (with – without) at Naomi and West Pointe à la Hache with a maximum capped at 2 *cm*.

differences between the two cases could have been over estimated. On day 25, water level differences in the upper basin were similar to those of day 20. However, in Barataria Bay, the impact of freshwater decreased, causing significant gradients with neighboring waters to the north. On day 30, all impact was reduced except at the diversion sites.

2.5 Impact of Diversion at Davis Pond

Another simulation run was made to simulate the impact of Davis Pond diversion on salinity distribution in the Barataria Basin the same 30-day period. The model was started from rest on July 7, 1999, and the first 5-day period was considered as the spin-up period. The model output was then compared to the case without the diversion. During this simulation, the freshwater diversion rate from the Davis Pond diversion site was fixed at either zero or $150\, m^3\, s^{-1}$ corresponding to 50% of the design maximum rate. Differences in salinity between the two cases (without Davis Pond diversion – with Davis Pond diversion) at five-day intervals are presented in Figure 2-20. On day 10 (HOUR 240), Barataria Waterway contained a nearly 1.5 ppt difference. When freshwater from Davis Pond reached Barataria Bay, the impact seemed to accelerate. It is clearly visible that high salinity difference values concentrate in the mid-bay. It is roughly estimated that the impact of freshwater diversion reaches the Gulf of Mexico in around 15 days after freshwater release. After about 15 days, the freshwater diversion seemed to impact most of the downstream region of the Barataria Basin except the eastern part of Barataria Bay and Caminada Bay. In the middle of Barataria Bay, the difference reached near 2 ppt. By day 25, most of the downstream basin was measurably impacted by freshwater diversion. Even after day 30, though, some isolated areas still remained without noticeable influence of the diversion due to morphological sheltering effect, i.e., in order to simulate this sheltering effect, detailed representation of morphological features of the basin is required. It is apparent that near the mouth and inside the bay, freshwater impact was reduced due to the strong tidal movement. Similar impact of freshwater diversion sites at Naomi and West Point a la Hache on salinity distribution in Barataria Bay was presented by Park (2002).

2.6 Summary and Conclusions

A high-resolution (O (100m)), integrated hydrology-hydrodynamic model of the Barataria Basin has been developed to simulate explicitly local hydrological cycle over the surrounding drainage basin and hydrodynamics within the basin in response to hydrological, tidal and wind forcing. A flood event due to the tropical storm Allison in June 2001 provided a rare opportunity to test the model. In the previous chapter, it was shown that the integrated model appears to be able to capture a significant portion of the observed sea-level variations during the flood.

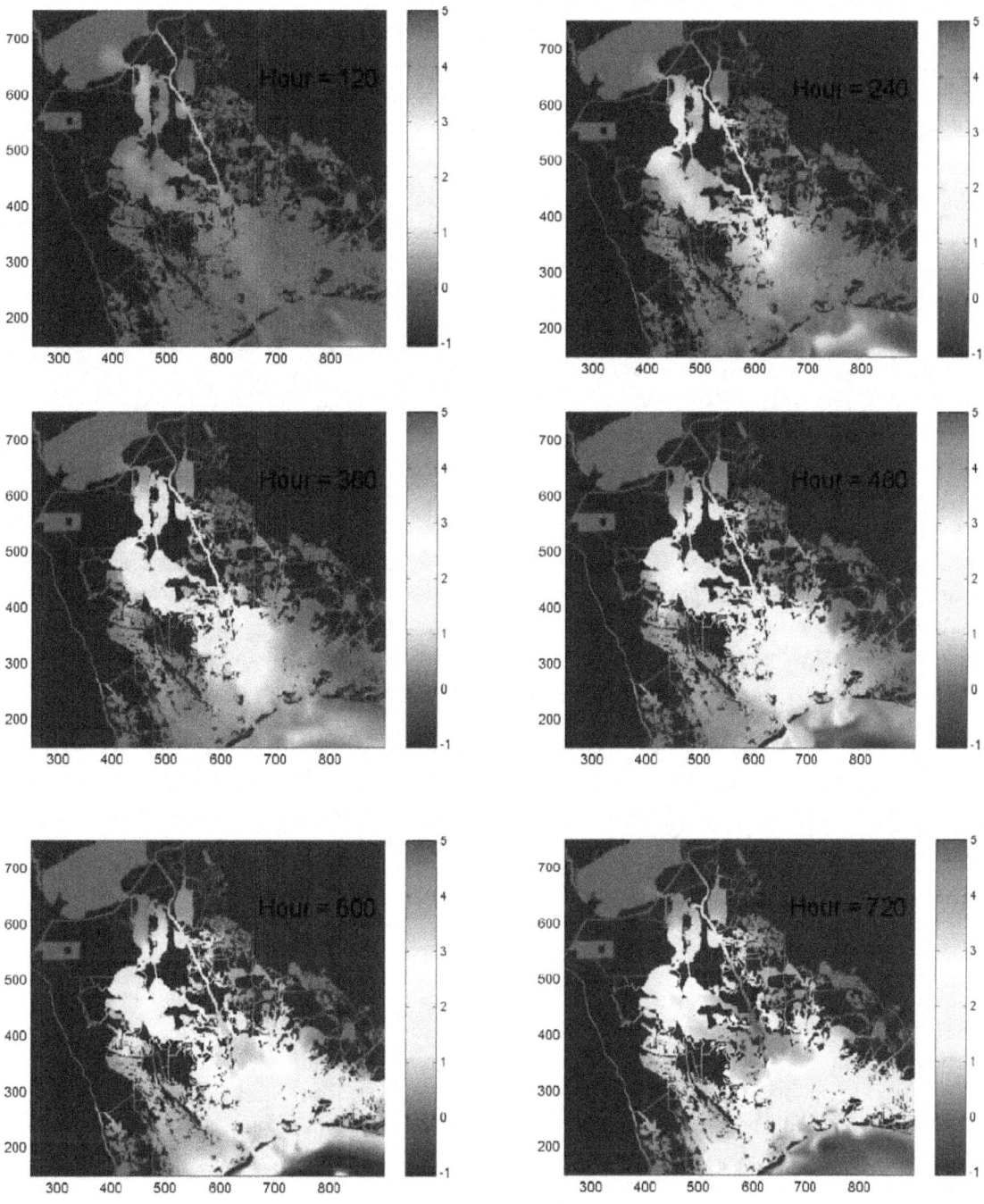

Figure. 2-20. Simulated salinity differences (ppt) between with and without Davis Pond diversion at 5-day intervals.

In this chapter, the integrated model was used to simulate a typical dry summer condition, namely the 30-day period during the summer of 1999. Despite the relatively crude salinity initial condition used (based on only eight observations), the model appears to do reasonable job of simulating time evolution of salinity fields inside the bay. The model was also used to simulate potential impact of freshwater diversions at Naomi, West Pointe à la Hache and at Davis Pond. Those simulation runs suggest that even at reasonable diversion rates, notable impacts on water level and salinity should be observable in the multiply connected channels through the marsh in the vicinity of operating diversion structures within several days of freshwater release, and after 15 days or so even in the downstream regions of the basin. The largest impact of diversions should be felt in the mid-bay region where the ambient salinity gradients are the steepest. It is notable that the speed associated with the propagation of diversion signal is much faster than the diffusion time-scale suggested for mixing of two water masses in an estuary (e. g., Elliot and Reid, 1976). Rather it appears that the signal of diversion propagates at shallow-water wave speed, like a tidal bore, due to its mass flux, consequently impacting depth-integrated salinity values downstream. It is interesting to note that even after day 30, some isolated areas within the bay still remain without noticeable influence of the diversion. Those observations highlight the need to use high model resolution, sufficiently high enough to resolve many of the important complex morphological features of the basin in order to achieve reasonable simulation capability of salinity distribution for morphologically complex basins such as Barataria Basin. Those simulation runs suggest a flushing time scale for the entire basin of 20~30 days, implying that not only the potential impact from any freshwater diversion but also any outside influence coming from the Gulf of Mexico would propagate throughout the basin within this time scale.

Those model simulation runs suggest that in order to achieve modeling capability usable for responsible management purposes, the model should; 1) account for local hydrological cycle including evaporation and precipitation, in particular local runoff from the surrounding drainage basins; 2) have high resolution in order to simulate very accurately salinity changes in the complex network of channels and bayous within the basin; 3) be thoroughly tested and calibrated against real observed data to be useful.

There still remain several important technical issues. One of them concerns the importance of three-dimensional effects in such shallow systems especially in deeper ship channels where some form of salt wedge might be expected during the flood tides. Another important issue is related to the specification of open boundary conditions. In this study, salinity values at open boundary were specified based on the estimation from Station S1. One alternative is to use data assimilation technique in that the observed salinity values at S1 can be inserted near S1.

Another critical issue is related to the availability of reliable precipitation data needed for hydrological input. Presently, in the vicinity the Barataria Basin, there are only two rain gauge stations are available with hourly measurements (they are Houma and New Orleans Airport). Considering the size of the surrounding drainage basin (6,300 km^2), precipitation estimates available only at those two stations won't be sufficient in order to provide detailed salinity distribution inside the bay. In the simulation during Tropical Storm Allison, we had to use rainfall data at New Orleans Airport to represent for the entire drainage basin. Although the results of the simulation were encouraging, considering the limitation of the rainfall estimates, actual spatial variability of rainfall during Allison was significant (Waple, et al., 2002). Therefore, significant improvement in our ability to estimate rainfall variability over the entire domain would be needed in order to achieve the desired goal of establishing simulation capability usable for management purposes. One potential way to overcome this problem is to utilize real-time rainfall estimation using geosynchronous satellite data recently developed (Vicente et al., 1998). The technique called the auto-estimator, uses the Geoestationary Operational Environmental Satellite-8 and -9 in the infrared (IR) band to compute real-time precipitation amounts based on a power-law regression algorithm. This regression is derived from a statistical analysis between surface radar-derived instantaneous rainfall estimates and satellite-derived IR cloud-top temperatures collocated in time and space. Although the estimates are indirect, the high frequency and high spatial resolution of the measurements, as well as the broad area coverage, make them uniquely complementary to rain gauge and radar measurements.

Verification studies are continuing. A verified and calibrated hydrology-hydrodynamic model will be useful for simulation of salinity changes in response to a variety of climactic conditions such as drought and flood. Those include impact of climatic changes not only on local hydrological cycle but also on the Mississippi River discharge, that would impact the basin via forcing coming from the Gulf of Mexico. For management purposes, the integrated model will be useful in simulating salinity alterations associated with the introduction of man-made freshwater diversions. With the availability of the integrated hydrology-hydrodynamic model, the foundation has been laid toward establishing modeling capability that could be usable for realistic management purposes.

CHAPTER 3

REFERENCES

Banas, P. J. 1978. An investigation of the circulation dynamics of a Louisiana bar-buit estuary. M.S. thesis, Louisiana State University, Baton Rouge, Louisiana 82 pp.

Barrett, B. B. 1971. Cooperative Gulf of Mexico estuarine inventory and study. Louisiana Phase II, Hydrology; Phase III, Sedimentology. LWFC, New Orleans, Louisiana.

Baumann, R. H. 1987. Chapter 2, Physical Variables. In: Conner W. H. and J. W. Day, Jr., editor. The Ecology of Barataria Basin, Louisiana: An estuarine profile. U.S. Fish and Wildlife Service Biological Report 85(7.13):165.

Beven, K. J. 2000. Rainfall-runoff modelling. Wiley. 360 pp.

Boris, J. P. and D. L. Book. 1973. Flux-corrected transport, I, SHAST: A fluid transport algorithm that works. J. Comput. Phys., 11:39-69.

Boshart, W. M. 1998. Naomi freshwater diversion. Louisiana Department of Natural Resources, Coastal Restoration Divesion. Three-year comprehensive monitoring report, Monitoring series No. BA-03-MSTY-1098-1. 22 pp.

Bowman, P. E., W. S. Perret, and J. E. Roussel. 1995. Freshwater introduction and implication for fisheries production in Louisiana. Baton Rouge, Louisiana: Department of Wildlife and Fisheries.

Butler, T. J. 1975. Aquatic metabolism and nutrient flux in a south Louisiana swamp and lake system. M.S. thesis. Department of Marine Sciences, Louisiana State University. 58 pp.

Byrne, P., M. Borengasser, G. Drew, R. A. Muller, B. L. Smith Jr. and C. Wax. 1976. Barataria Basin: Hydrologic and climatologic processes. Louisiana State University Center for Wetland Resources. Sea Grant Publ. No. LSU-T-76-010.

Camerlengo, A. L. and J. J. O'Brien. 1980. Open boundary conditions in rotating fluids. J. Comput. Phys., 35:12-35.

Colon, J. A. 1963. Seasonal variations in heat flux from the sea surface to the atmosphere over the Caribbean Sea. J. Geophys. Res., 68:1421-1430.

Dyer, K. R. 1973. Estuaries: A physical introduction. New York, NY: John Wiley. 140 pp.

Elliott, A. J. and R. O. Reid. 1976. Salinity induced horizontal estuarine circulation. Journal of the Waterways Harbors and Coastal Engineering Division. WW4:425-442.

Gagliano, S. M., P. Culley, D. W. Earle, P. King, C. Latiolais, P. Light, A. Rowland, R. Shlemon, and J. L. van Beek. 1973. Hydrologic and geologic studies of coastal Louisiana-environmental atlas and multiuse management plan for South-Central Louisiana. Report No. 18, Volume I:132.

Galtsoff, P. S., 1964. The American oyster, *Crasostrea Virginica* (Gmelin). Fish. Bull. Vol. 64. U.S. Dept. of the Interior, Fish and Wildlife Service.

Grammeltvedt, A. 1969. A survey of finite-difference schemes for the primitive equations for a barotropic fluid. Monthly Weather Review, 97:384-404.

Hacker, S. 1973. Transport phenomena in Estuaries. Ph.D. dissertation, Louisiana State University, Baton Rouge, Louisiana. 186 pp.

Hasumi, H. and N. Suginohara. 1999. Sensitivity of a global circulation model to tracer advection schemees. J. Phys. Oceanogr., 29:2730-2740.

Henry, W. K. 1979. Some aspects of the cold fronts in the Gulf of Mexico. Mon. Weather. Rev., 101:1078-1082.

Howard, P. C. 1982. Quatre Bayou Pass, Louisiana: Analysis of currents, sediment and history. M.S. thesis, Department of Geology, Louisiana University, Baton Rouge, Louisiana. 111 pp.

Hsu, S. A. 1988. Coastal meteorology. San Diego, CA: Academic Press. 260 pp.

Hsu, S. A. 1997. Effects of cold air outbreaks on evaporation and heat loss from three regions in the Gulf of Mexico. Gulf of Mexico Science, 2:71-76.

Huh, O. K., L. J. Rouse, Jr., and N. D. Walker. 1984. Cold air outbreaks over the northwest Florida continental shelf: Heat flux processes and hydrographic changes. J. Geophys. Res., 89:717-726.

Inoue, M., W. J. Wiseman, Jr., and D. Park. 1998. Coastal marine environmental modeling. U.S. Dept. of the Interiors, Minerals Management Service, Gulf of Mexico OCS Region, New Orleans, Louisiana. OCS Study MMS 98-0052. 133 pp.

Inoue, M. and W. J. Wiseman, Jr. 2000. Transport, stirring and mixing process in a Louisiana estuary: A model study. Estuarine. Coastal and Shelf Science, 50:449-466.

Inoue, M., W. J. Wiseman, Jr., D. Park, D. Justic, and G. Stone. 2001. Dispersion in broad, shallow estuaries: A model study. U.S. Dept. of the Interior, Minerals Management Service, Gulf of Mexico OCS Region, New Orleans, Louisiana. OCS Study MMS 2001-054. 54 pp.

Kjerfve, B. 1973. Dynamics of the water surface in a bar-built estuary. Ph.D. dissertation, Louisiana State University, Baton Rouge, Louisiana. 90 pp.

Kjerfve, B. 1975. Tide and fair-weather effects in a bar-built Louisiana estuary. Estuarine Research, 2:47-62.

Leendertse, J. J. 1967. Aspects of a computational model for long period water wave propagation. RM-5294-PR, Rand Corporation, Santa Monica, CA. 165 pp.

Leonard, B. P. 1979. A stable and accurate convective modeling procedure based on quadratic upstream interpolation. Comput. Methods Appl. Mech. Eng., 19:59-98.

Leonard, B. P., M. K. MacVean, and A. P. Lock. 1993. Positivity-preserving numerical schemes for multidimensional advection. NASA Tech. Memo. 106055, ICOMP-93-05. 62 pp.

Light P., R. J. Shelemon, P.T. Culley, and N. A. Roques. 1973. Hydrologic models for the Barataria-Terrebonne area, south-central Louisiana. Hydrologic and geologic studies of coastal Louisiana. No. 16, 43 pp.

Louisiana Coastal Wetlands Conservation and Restoration Task. 1993. Louisiana Coastal Wetlands Conservation Plan, Barataria Basin, Appendix D. 149 pp.

Marmer, H. A. 1954. Tides and sea level in Gulf of Mexico. U.S. Fish and Wildlife Service. Fish. Bull., 89:101-118.

Melancon, E., Jr., T. Soniat, V. Cheramie, M. Lagarde, R. Dugas, and J. Barras. 1994. Barataria-Terrebonne National Estuary Program: The oyster resources zones within Louisiana and Terrebonne estuaries. BTNET-15, Barataria-Terrebonne National Estuary Program. 184 pp.

Mesinger, F. and A. Arakawa. 1976. Numerical methods used in atmospheric models. GARP Pub. Ser. 17, World Meteorological Organization, Geneva, Switzerland. 64 pp.

Muller, R. A. 1975. Freshwater potensial in the Louisiana coastal marshes and estuaries. Department of Geography and Anthropology, Louisiana State University, Baton Rouge, Louisiana. Geoscience and Man, 12:1-7.

Park, D. H. 1998. A modeling study of the Barataria Basin system. M.S. thesis, Louisiana State University, Baton Rouge, Louisiana. 133 pp.

Park, D. H. 2002. Hydrodynamics and freshwater dispersion within Barataria Basin. Ph.D. dissertation, Louisiana State University, Baton Rouge, Louisiana. 107 pp.

72

Raudkivi, A. J. 1979. Hydrology: An advanced introduction to hydrological processes and modelling. Pergamon Press. 479 pp.

Roberts, D. W., J. L. van Beck, S. Fournet, and S. J. Williams, 1992. Adatement of wetland loss in Louisiana through diversions of Mississippi River water using siphons. Open-File Report 92-274, U. S. Geological Survey, Reston, Virginia, 54 pp.

Roll, H. U. 1965. Physics of the marine atmosphere. New York: Academic Press. 426 pp.

Schroeder, W. W. and W. J. Wiseman Jr. 1986. Low-frequency shelf-estuarine exchange processes in Mobile Bay and other estuarine systems on the northern Gulf of Mexico. In: Wolfe, D. A. ed., Estuarine Variability. Orlando, Florida. Academic Press, Inc. 509 pp.

Sklar, F. H. 1983. Water budget, benthological characterization, and simulation of aquatic material flows in a Louisiana freshwater swamps. Ph.D. dissertation, Louisiana State University, Baton Rouge, Louisiana. 280 pp.

Smith, K. B. Katsaros, W. A. Oost, and P. G. Mestayer. 1994. The impact of the HEXOS programme. Preprints, Second Int. Conf. Air-Sea Interaction and on Meteorology and Oceanography of the Coastal Zone, Lisbon, Portugal, Amer. Metero. Soc. Pp. 226-227.

Smolarkiewcz, P. K. 1984. A fully multidimensional positive definite advection transport algorithm with small implicit diffusion. J. Comput. Phys., 54:325-362.

Swarzenski, C. M., A. N. Traver, and C. K. Labbe. 1999. The Gulf Intercoastal Waterway as a conduit of freshwater and sediments to coastal Louisiana wetlands, 1999. Poster Presentation.

Swenson, E. M. and R. E. Turner 1998. Past, present and probable future salinity variations in the Barataria Basin System. Prepared for Coastal Restoration and Management, Louisiana Department of Natural Resources. 112 pp.

Takacs, L. L. 1985. A two-step scheme for the advection equation with minimized dissipation and dispersion errors. Mon. Wea. Rev., 113:1050-1065.

Turner, R. E. 1990. Landscape development and coastal wetland losses in the northern Gulf of Mexico. American Zoologist, 30:89-105.

Van Sickle, V. R., B. B. Barrett, and T. B. Ford. 1976. Barataria Basin: Salinity changes and oyster distribution. Louisiana State University Center for Wetland Resources. Sea Grant Publ. No. LSU-T-76-02.

Viessman, W., Jr., G. L. Lewis, and J. W. Knapp. 1989. Introduction to hydrology. Harper & Row Publishers. 780 pp.

Vincente, G. A., R. A. Scofield, and W. P. Menzel. 1998. The operational GOES infrared rainfall estimation technique. Bulletin of the American Meteorological Society, 79, 1883-1898.

von Arx, W. S. 1950. The Barataria Bay model. Unpublished report to the Freeport Sulphur Company.

Walesh, S. G. 1989. Urban surface water management. A Willy-Interscience Publication. 518 pp.

Waple, A. M., J. H. Larimore, M. S. Halpert, G. D. Bell, W. Higgins, B. Lyon, M. J. Menne, K. L. Gleason, R. C. Schnell, J. R. Christy, W. Thiaw, W. J. Wright, M. J. Salinger, L. Alexander, R. S. Stone, and S. J. Camargo. 2002. Climate Assessment for 2001. Bulletin of the American Meteorological Society, 83, S1-S62.

Wax, C. L., M. J. Borengasser, and R. A. Muller. 1978. Barataria Basin: Synoptic weather types and environmental response. Center for Wetland Resources, Louisiana State University, Baton Rouge, Louisiana. Sea Grant Publication Number LSU-T-78-001.

Wiseman, W. J., Jr., and E. M. Swenson. 1989. Modelling the effects of produced water discharges on estuarine salinity. Part of "Environmental impact of produced water discharges in coastal Louisiana." 287 pp.

Wiseman, W. J., Jr., E. M. Swenson, and F. J. Kelly. 1990. Control of estuarine salinities by coastal ocean salinity. In: Cheng, R. T. ed. Residual Currents and Long-term Transport Processes, Coastal and Estuarine Studies. Springer-Verlag, New York, 38:184-193.

Wiseman, W. J., Jr., E. M. Swenson, and J. Power. 1990. Salinity trends in Louisiana estuaries. Estuaries, 13(3):265-271.

Wiseman, W. J., Jr., and M. Inoue. 1993. Salinity variations in two Louisiana estuaries. In: Magoon, O. T., W. S. Wilson, H. Converse and L. T. Tobin, eds. Proceedings Coastal Zone '93, 8th Symposium on Coastal and Ocean Management, New Orleans, Louisiana, July 19-23. 1:1,230-1,242.

Wiseman, W. J., Jr., and M. Inoue. 1994. Salinity variability and transport processes. In: Roberts, H. H. Critical physical processes of wetland loss. Final Report to U.S. Geological Survey. Coastal Studies Institute, Louisiana State University, Baton Rouge, LA. Pp. 3.1-3.31.

Wiseman, W. J., Jr. 1996. Unpublished lecture note *Estuarine Dynamics*." Louisiana State University, Coastal Studies Institute. 54 pp.

The Department of the Interior Mission

As the Nation's principal conservation agency, the Department of the Interior has responsibility for most of our nationally owned public lands and natural resources. This includes fostering sound use of our land and water resources; protecting our fish, wildlife, and biological diversity; preserving the environmental and cultural values of our national parks and historical places; and providing for the enjoyment of life through outdoor recreation. The Department assesses our energy and mineral resources and works to ensure that their development is in the best interests of all our people by encouraging stewardship and citizen participation in their care. The Department also has a major responsibility for American Indian reservation communities and for people who live in island territories under U.S. administration.

The Minerals Management Service Mission

As a bureau of the Department of the Interior, the Minerals Management Service's (MMS) primary responsibilities are to manage the mineral resources located on the Nation's Outer Continental Shelf (OCS), collect revenue from the Federal OCS and onshore Federal and Indian lands, and distribute those revenues.

Moreover, in working to meet its responsibilities, the **Offshore Minerals Management Program** administers the OCS competitive leasing program and oversees the safe and environmentally sound exploration and production of our Nation's offshore natural gas, oil and other mineral resources. The MMS **Minerals Revenue Management** meets its responsibilities by ensuring the efficient, timely and accurate collection and disbursement of revenue from mineral leasing and production due to Indian tribes and allottees, States and the U.S. Treasury.

The MMS strives to fulfill its responsibilities through the general guiding principles of: (1) being responsive to the public's concerns and interests by maintaining a dialogue with all potentially affected parties and (2) carrying out its programs with an emphasis on working to enhance the quality of life for all Americans by lending MMS assistance and expertise to economic development and environmental protection.